Ritual and Democracy

Ritual and Democracy

Protests, Publics and Performances

Edited by
Sarah M. Pike, Jone Salomonsen, and
Paul-François Tremlett

e؟uinox

SHEFFIELD UK   BRISTOL CT

Published by Equinox Publishing Ltd.

UK: Office 415, The Workstation, 15 Paternoster Row, Sheffield,
        South Yorkshire S1 2BX
USA: ISD, 70 Enterprise Drive, Bristol, CT 06010

www.equinoxpub.com

First published 2020

British Library Cataloguing-in-Publication Data
A catalogue record for this book is available from the British Library.

ISBN-13   978 1 78179 974 1   (hardback)
            978 1 78179 975 8   (paperback)
            978 1 78179 976 5   (ePDF)

Library of Congress Cataloging-in-Publication Data
Names: Pike, Sarah M., 1959- editor. | Salomonsen, Jone, 1956- editor. |
    Tremlett, Paul-François, editor.
Title: Ritual and democracy : protests, publics and performances / edited
    by Sarah M. Pike, Jone Salomonsen, and Paul-François Tremlett.
Description: Sheffield, South Yorkshire ; Bristol, CT : Equinox Publishing
    Ltd., 2020. | Includes bibliographical references and index. | Summary:
    "This interdisciplinary and theoretically innovative edited volume,
    contains seven research rich chapters exploring and critically assess
    conjunctions of ritual and democracy in a wide range of cultural and
    geographic contexts. The volume emerged out of a workshop held at the
    Open University in London in 2015, organized as part of the
    international research project, "Reassembling Democracy: Ritual as
    Cultural Resource (REDO)," funded by the Norwegian Research Council. The
    authors of these chapters analyze instances of collective mourning and
    commemoration, festivals, ecological and political protest, and
    pilgrimage, and spiritual dance, through attention to the complex
    intersections of ritual, politics, and democracy"-- Provided by
    publisher.
Identifiers: LCCN 2019038789 (print) | LCCN 2019038790 (ebook) | ISBN
    9781781799741 (hardback) | ISBN 9781781799758 (paperback) | ISBN
    9781781799765 (ebook)
Subjects: LCSH: Political customs and rites. | Religion and politics. |
    Democracy.
Classification: LCC GN492.3 .R56 2020 (print) | LCC GN492.3 (ebook) | DDC
    306.2--dc23
LC record available at https://lccn.loc.gov/2019038789
LC ebook record available at https://lccn.loc.gov/2019038790

Typeset by S.J.I. Services, New Delhi, India

Contents

Acknowledgements

The editors would like to thank the Norwegian Research Council and The Open University (UK) for their support, participants in the research project "Reassembling Democracy: Ritual as Cultural Resource" for four years of excellent and inspiring conversation and critique, and the fine folks of Equinox for making this book possible: Janet Joyce, Valerie Hall, Sarah Lee, and Chas S. Clifton.

Introduction

Sarah M. Pike, Jone Salomonsen, and Paul-François Tremlett

Ritual acts and performances construct, reveal, and mobilise pervasive cultural and political resources. Within the complex set of language, forms of expression, norms, values, ideas, and behaviours, ritual is a privileged medium in the articulation of memory, expression of identity, and response to change. Yet ritual is not merely a mobiliser, constructed by the social as a precondition to the development and stability of society, it is also a catalyst for change. Creative responses to crises triggered by the dynamics of contemporary global transformation commonly involve culturally and religiously informed ritualized actions. As people engage in such activities, they build new conditions for political engagement and action, acquire and demonstrate novel competencies, and continuously renegotiate social identities, thereby transforming the cultural and political processes that constitute society. This volume focuses on selected rituals that arise out of social and environmental activism and grassroots political change. It explores the extent to which they shape the future, create community, open out new political spaces, generate new subjectivities and restructure society in a global context.

Contemporary individuals and communities are currently faced with complex crises and changes pertaining to culture, nature, religion, language, politics, media, economy, and technology. The research presented in this volume assumes that in dealing with these transformations, they mobilize cultural resources that may be drawn from varied and competing knowledge and experience bases. As individuals participate in their societies and other assemblages, interactions between persons, communities and environments mobilize larger social fields. While potentially enriching democratic processes, they may also bring about challenges to existing political structures. In cases of innovation and contestation, ritual behaviours habituated by previous cultural repertoires seem to be utilized—deliberately or casually—by explicit design or by responsive borrowing. In turn, these behaviours are disseminated and adapted in other contexts, shaping participants and societies as they too are shaped by varying circumstances, conditions and contexts. Cultural resources become visible in ritual acts, which in turn become new cultural resources, assembling and re-assembling people and societies at once as actors and as acted-upon. Hence, these chapters also respond to the following questions: Are ritual gestures and modes of organization and expression merely effective mobilizers for social change (or stability), or are they constitutive of how society changes and develops? How can we know the difference? What models and theories can best explain ritual resource-fulness? Is ritual agency gendered? By exploring selected ritual activities in our case studies, we will address these and other questions concerning the complex relationship between ritual and democracy.

The theoretical framework for this volume is informed by Ritual Studies approaches and debates. For instance, many of the chapters build on Bruce Kapferer's recognition that rituals are 'not merely representative of changes, they effect them' (2004: 43), and also on Bradshaw and Melloh's claim that 'ritual facilitates meaningful social change by focusing on society's general conceptions of the order of existence with the actual circumstances of its daily life' (Bradshaw and Melloh 2007: 168). Implicit here is a tension that has generated considerable debate among scholars interested in the category of 'ritual': ritual activity constitutes a mechanism both for stability and for sudden and radical change. It is in light of this dynamic that the volume addresses the ways in which ritual acts recombine and mobilise cultural resources in order to better understand society and its constituent assem-blages and wider processes of change. Whereas Bruce Kapferer (2004) has theorized ritual efficacy by analyzing strongly framed, magical rites in which change is mainly measured individually (social status) or therapeu-tically (personal well-being), we interrogate new ritual forms emerging in non-magical global society and varied popular contexts.

The volume also arises from and addresses our shared interests in the nature and enactment of embodied society and culture. In this context, we draw on Bruno Latour's 'actor network theory' and its application to 'reas-sembling the social' (2005). We propose that cultural or religious ritual is not only representative of the social, but integral to its embodied constitu-tion and reconstitution. This analytical stance is also supported by Richard Sennett, who argues that ritual may play a key role in developing peace-ful co-habitation in a multicultural society exactly because it instils skill in its participants (2012). However, as religious pluralization becomes one of the most characteristic features of the cultural conditions driving societal change today, ritual will embody pluralism in its own right and design new inclusive arenas for dialogue and collaboration on the one hand and tribal, identity-focused initiatives on the other. Increased ritual pluralization seems to be occurring simultaneously with an increased bifurcation and politicisation of religious traditions.

The aim of *Ritual and Democracy: Protests, Publics and Performances* is the comparative scholarly analysis of how accelerating ritual pluralisation and ritual mobilization among new stakeholders are creating new cultural conditions for community building, multicultural co-habitation, public mourning, direct democracy and religious dialogue, as well as confrontation and contestation within and between societal groups. The investigation of these processes is accomplished in the following chapters by detailed studies of local ritual pluralization strategies and ritual responses to social and environmental crises in Europe, Asia, the Middle East and the Americas.

Overview of the Chapters

This volume is divided into three closely connected parts: Protests, Publics, and Performances. The three chapters in the first part of the book focused on 'Protests', explore and analyse three very different kinds of protest activity in the early twenty-first century in three different parts of the world: the anti-government protests in Istanbul, the Occupy Democracy protests in London, and the Charlie Hebdo cartoons and killings in Paris and protests in Pakistan.

Part I: Protests

The three chapters that constitute Part I approach the political, and in particular protest, as the moment that deconstructs the social imaginary and its conception of itself as complete, stable, and enduring. Ritual is precisely the technology that both affirms the social and forms the singularity that explodes it. The section begins with Agnes Czajka's chapter, which offers a brief overview of the recent struggles over democracy in Turkey, focusing on the 2013 Gezi Park protests and the attempted coup in 2016. Czajka foregrounds two performative repertoires that emerged during the Gezi Park protests and in the aftermath of the attempted coup: the communal earth *iftars* first organized during the Gezi Park protests and held annually since, and the democracy vigil that followed the attempted coup. In exploring these two repertoires, the chapter suggests that the earth *iftars*, which draw on a 'religious', 'Muslim' ritual, offer a more radically open, inclusive and indeed 'democratic' articulation of democracy than the 'secular', 'nationalist' vigil avowedly staged in defence of democracy. The chapter concludes with a brief consideration of Jacques Derrida's articulation of democracy and deconstruction, suggesting that the deconstructive framework and Derrida's conception of democracy-to-come offer a way of grasping what might, at first glance, seem like a counterintuitive argument, namely that the performance of a 'religious' ritual has greater democratic potential than the 'secular' performance explicitly staged in defence of democracy.

The work accomplished in Czajka's chapter paves the way for a further unsettling of taken-for-granted assumptions about the religious and the political, this time regarding the sites and occasions of political agency. Paul-François Tremlett and then Zaki Nahaboo attend closely to the materiality of protests, concentrating on acts of iconoclasm, the burning of effigies, and the political agency of things. Tremlett begins his chapter with a specific moment of political protest that took place in London in 2014, organized by a group called Occupy Democracy. The protest was marked by the iconoclastic destruction of protest material culture by heritage wardens and police. Tremlett draws from Durkheim's theory of totemism and Bennett's vitalist account of politics and their conceptions of energy, contrasting the ontologies of the social and of the subject they presuppose and arguing that they have important consequences for contemporary imaginaries of politics and political agency. Nahaboo's chapter revisits the 2015 'Je suis Charlie' mobilizations in France and subsequent protests in Pakistan. Nahaboo employs a performative conception of ritual to explore the political dimensions of social movements, before analysing certain ritual enactments within the Je suis Charlie movement, notably in relation to Marianne, the national symbol of the French republic. He then traces a response to this ambivalent expression of free speech through the destruction of the former editor-in-chief of Charlie Hebdo, Stéphane Charbonnier, in effigy. By tracking the materialization of free speech in objects which are differently revered and destroyed, Nahaboo is able to demonstrate the political agency of objects in the constitution of the political.

Part II: Publics

The second part of this volume, 'Publics', features two case studies that explore the ways in which different publics are constituted through strategies of ritualization in the context of changing demographics and relationships to national identity. The two cases include contemporary ritual practices, often improvised and revised from older traditions: Norwegian pilgrimages and Protestant Christian liturgy in Copenhagen.

Marion Grau's combined theological inquiry and ethnographic study of contemporary Norwegian pilgrims draws on contemporary theoretical understandings of multispeces networks of relationships in the writings of Bruno Latour, Donna Haraway, and Anna Tsing. Grau traces the weave of narratives around land and sea pilgrimages along St. Olav Ways in Norway, and the Olavsfestdagene (Feast days of St. Olav) where the religious and political heritage of St. Olav, saint and king of Norway, is narrated, performed, and reshaped. In Grau's study of the 'pilgrimage network' around St. Olav, she explores the ways in which pilgrimage and festival are sites where pilgrims, festival performers, and audiences renegotiate the socio-political, economic, ecological, and religious narratives that have shaped contemporary Norway: their relationship to nature and landscape, the past, oil wealth, recent increases in immigration, and the aftermath of domestic terror. As pilgrims' bodies move across land and seascapes, they create new stories and new meanings and improvise on traditional narratives. Her chapter lays the groundwork for a polydox theology of migration and pilgrimage through space and time in Norway, through changing landscapes and narratives of national identity that argue for an expanding planetary sense of democracy that includes humans, animals and landscapes.

Gitte Buch-Hansen's contribution is also situated within the context of immigration in contemporary Northern Europe and also focuses on embodied ritual actions and experiences. During the mid-2000s, the immigration of refugees—primarily from Iran, Iraq, Syria, and Afghanistan—occasioned a major political and cultural crisis in the former ethnically, culturally, and religiously homogeneous Danish society. As 78 per cent of ethnic Danes are members of the Lutheran Evangelical Church of Denmark, this has been played out in the field of religion and taken the form of a—potential—conflict between a traditionally Christian culture and Islam. Officially, the position of the national church with regard to Islam is one of interreligious dialogue. In fact, hybrid identities are *not* welcomed by Danish politicians who—in spite of the demand for cultural integration—see immigrants' and refugees' conversions as strategic attempts to improve their possibilities for residence. Buch-Hansen's case study focuses on an exception to this hostile climate, the Apostles' Church in the centre of Copenhagen, that welcomes converts as well as Muslim refugees and migrants in the life of their church. Buch-Hansen's fieldwork focuses on patterns of food consumption and the rituals associated with eating within the congregation. Her discussion of these rituals draws on the work of literary critic Julia Kristeva, who argued that the consumption of food was the most basic way that societies produce identity, in-groups, and social borders. The chapter sheds light on the way that cultural and religious conflicts and tensions were made manageable through the Eucharist. However, as the participants took part in the traditional Christian ritual, the Eucharist also changed its meaning and theology for the congregation. Her study exemplifies how—through the creation of a heterotopic space—traditional rituals may help the re-signification of social space and expanded meanings of democratic practice.

Part III: Performances

The third and final part of this book includes an ethnographic research project on contemporary collective dancing in Paris and a study of indigenous festivals in the United Kingdom, United States, and Norway. These two chapters set out to explore the ways in which democracy is both constituted and contested through performative actions such as dance and music.

In 'Dances of Self-development as a Resource for Participatory Democracy', Michael Houseman and Marie Mazzella di Bosco explore ritualization with a sense of what potential models for democracy might emerge from contemporary collective dance in urban France. Based on participatory fieldwork undertaken mostly in France, this chapter explores the political dimensions of collective dance practices pursued in the spirit of self-discovery and personal transformation (5 Rhythms, Movement Medicine, Biodanza, etc.). For Houseman and Mazzella di Bosco, collective dance events are not instances of political activism in and of themselves, nor are they organized according to democratic principles. However, they call into play moral and social values that are consonant with the principles that democratically inspired political actions, such as those discussed in earlier chapters, seek to put into effect. In this respect, these dances are not, as one might suspect, reducible to the consumption of a resource for individual self-fulfilment. Houseman and Mazzella di Bosco argue that like many other contemporary 'alternative' or 'spiritual' initiatives, these activities involve participants in extra-ordinary yet lived-through situations that enact a special mode of sociability, many aspects of which are immediately relevant to the functioning of social movements based on participatory democratic principles. They conclude that while personal development has often been seen as a 'by-product' of radically democratic practice, the reverse can also be true. By affording participants with ritual experiences in which individual autonomy and collective solidarity are made interdependent, these practices can be a resource for democratic commitment in the political sphere.

Graham Harvey's contribution also explores performances that constitute and negotiate collective identity, but in the context of international

Indigenous music festivals. Like many of the authors in this volume, he expands democracy to include other-than-human persons. His chapter, 'Trans-Indigenous Festivals: Democracy and Emplacement', explores indigenous cultural festivals that attract international performers and audiences and are both local and global. Harvey's cases include events as diverse as First Nation reserve powwows, the annual Riddu Riđđu festival organized by Sámi in arctic Norway, and the biennial Origins Festival in London. These events include diverse genres of music, dance, film, theatre, costume, workshops and youth camps. Harvey considers the varied ways in which such festivals extend democratic possibilities for participants and their communities. Such possibilities begin with the recovery of cultural pride even while at the margins of dominant (and dominating) societies. They include opportunities to debate issues confronting many Indigenous peoples. At the same time, these festivals push the notion of place as larger-than-human or multispecies community. Harvey argues that trans-Indigenous approaches to democracy may be seen in efforts to increase human inclusivity and in the inclusion of other-than-human persons. It is the pervasive Indigenous understanding of emplacement that most radically confronts cultural assumptions that place is mere scenery or a resource for exploitation.

Taken as a whole, this volume offers an original, theoretically informed contribution to contemporary debates about ritual, politics and democracy. It is international in scope with wide-ranging case studies analysing the complex relationship between ritual and democracy in United Kingdom, Turkey, Pakistan, France, Norway, and Denmark. As an interdisciplinary group of researchers with interconnected research questions on ritual, democracy, and religion, we tap our rich experiences through the use of different research methods from the disciplines of anthropology, sociology, geography, religious studies, theology, political science, history and philosophy. All of the chapters entail (at least an element of) fieldwork involving participant-observation and structured or semi-structured interviews with members of selected communities, movements, assemblages and/or church groups. The practices of reflexivity, dialogue and collaborative comparison of multi-sited ethnographic fieldwork make the performance, utilization, and production of ethnography most suited to careful data collection, analysis and theorization about ritual's role in democratization processes in a rapidly changing world.

References

Bradshaw, Paul and Melloh, John (2007), *Foundations in Ritual Studies*. London: SPCK Publishing.

Kapferer, Bruce (2004), 'Ritual Dynamics and Virtual Practice: Beyond Representation and Meaning.' *Social Analysis*, 48: 33–54. https://doi.org/10.3167/015597704782352591.

Latour, Bruno (2005), *Reassembling the Social: An Introduction to Actor-Network-Theory*. Oxford: Oxford University Press. https://doi.org/10.1108/eoi.2008.27.3.307.2.

Sennett, Richard (2012), *Together: The Rituals, Pleasures and Politics of Cooperation*. New Haven: Yale University Press. https://doi.org/10.3917/mana.153.0344.

About the Editors

Sarah M. Pike is professor of comparative religion and chair of the Department of Comparative Religion and Humanities at California State University, Chico. She has written numerous books, articles, and book chapters on contemporary Paganism, ritual, the New Age movement, the Burning Man festival, spiritual dance, environmental activism, the ancestral skills movement, and youth culture. Her most recent book is *For the Wild: Ritual and Commitment in Radical Eco-Activism* (University of California Press, 2017), an ethnographic study of radical environmental and animal rights activism, ritual, and youth culture.

Jone Salomonsen is professor of theology on the Faculty of Theology at the University of Oslo. She is the project manager for the Norwegian Research Council-funded project Reassembling Democracy: Ritual as Cultural Resource. Her teaching areas include contemporary religion, method, ritual studies, constructive theology, and feminist theory.

Paul-François Tremlett is a senior lecturer in religious studies at The Open University. He is interested in religions and processes of rapid religious and social change. Publications include *Claude Lévi-Strauss: The Structuring Mind* (Equinox, 2008) as well as the co-edited volumes *Re-Writing Culture in Taiwan* (Routledge 2008) and *Edward Burnett Tylor, Religion and Culture* (Bloomsbury 2017). He is co-editor of the Bloomsbury book series Studies in Religion, Space and Place.

Part 1
Protests

1. Rituals of Resistance and the Struggle over Democracy in Turkey[1]

Agnes Czajka

The 2013 Gezi Park protests and the 2016 coup attempt in Turkey were watershed moments in recent struggles over Turkish democracy. Both made use of and gave rise to performative repertoires that unmistakably revealed the existence of competing conceptions of democracy in Turkey. This chapter explores the manner in which two of these repertoires—the *yeryüzü iftarları* (earth *iftars*) and *demokrasi nöbeti* (democracy vigil)—performatively disclose two distinct and indeed, irreconcilable, variations on democracy.

The chapter first offers a brief overview of the recent struggles over democracy in Turkey, focusing on the 2013 Gezi Park protests and the attempted coup in 2016. It then foregrounds two performative repertoires that emerged during the Gezi Park protests and in the aftermath of the attempted coup: the communal earth *iftars* first organized during the Gezi Park protests, and held annually since; and the democracy vigil that followed the attempted coup. I suggest that the earth *iftars*, which draw on a 'religious', 'Muslim' ritual, offer a more radically open, inclusive and indeed 'democratic' articulation of democracy than the 'secular', 'nationalist' vigil avowedly staged in defence of democracy. The chapter concludes with a brief consideration of Jacques Derrida's articulation of democracy and deconstruction, suggesting that the deconstructive framework and Derrida's conception of democracy-to-come offer a way of grasping what might, at first glance, seem like a counterintuitive argument—namely, that the performance of a 'religious' ritual has

1   This chapter is based on two presentations that I gave to researchers and guests of the Reassembling Democracy: Ritual as Resource (REDO) project, first in London in September 2015 and then in Oslo in February 2017. My attendance at both events was generously supported by the REDO project, for which I am extremely grateful. I am also indebted to the discussants, and all those who attended the events and provided valuable feedback on drafts of the chapter. During this time, I was also working on *Democracy and Justice: Reading Derrida in Istanbul* (2017). Some of the arguments I make in this chapter—on deconstruction, democracy and the earth *iftars*—are also developed in that book.

greater democratic potential than the 'secular' performance explicitly staged in defence of democracy.

From Gezi to Coup: The Struggle Over Turkish Democracy

Comprehensive accounts of the Gezi Park protests, which started in earnest on 27 May 2013, are numerous (Benlisoy 2013; Czajka 2017; Erbil 2013; Sönmez 2013; Tuğal 2013; Yaman 2013), as are accounts of the struggle over Turkish democracy since the coming to power of the ruling *Adalet ve Kalkınma Partisi* (AKP) in 2002 (Hale 2010; Heper 2010; Sözen 2014; Tep, 2015). The Gezi Park protests started rather innocuously, sparked by the controversial 'Taksim Pedestrianization Project' that, among other things, proposed the rebuilding of the Halil Pasha Artillery Barracks also known as *Topçu Kışlası* ('Taksim military barracks') and their conversion into a luxury hotel, residences, and shopping complex. The stated aim of the pedestrianization project, announced in September 2011 by the AKP-controlled Metropolitan Municipality of Istanbul, was to facilitate freer and more comfortable public access to Taksim Square. But the proposal was harshly and publically criticized as it entailed the destruction of Gezi Park, one of the few remaining green spaces in central Istanbul. Many saw the project as part of the government's drive towards unrestrained and irresponsible construction, and its attempt to depoliticise and desocialize one of the most vibrant areas of Istanbul, and a frequent site of protests (Taksim Meydanı 2011).

Opponents of the project, which included a wide cross-section of NGOs, labour unions, professional and business associations, and resident and community organizations, came together under the banner of 'Taksim Solidarity' and publically criticized both the project and the lack of accompanying consultation. Yet the municipal government pressed on. It awarded the redevelopment contract to Kalyon Construction, a corporation with close ties to the AKP, and gave the go-ahead for the project, which started in October 2012. The plans to raze Gezi Park were given final approval in February 2013. When construction workers attempted to enter Gezi Park on the evening of 27 May 2013 to begin uprooting trees, members of Taksim Solidarity, who had been safeguarding the park for a few months fearing potential incursions, occupied the park, forming a human chain to prevent its destruction.

Whilst the occupation garnered some media attention, it was then Prime Minister Recep Tayyip Erdoğan's televised reaction, and the subsequent brutality with which the police attempted to disperse protesters, that transformed the Gezi Park protests into the largest in recent Turkish history. On

29 May, speaking at a ceremony inaugurating the equally controversial construction of a third bridge across the Bosphorus Strait, and referring to the Gezi Park protesters, Erdoğan declared that, 'irrespective of what a few hoodlums want, we have made our decision and we will follow through' (Ne Yaparsanız 2013). Enraged by Erdoğan's remarks, thousands of Istanbulites arrived in Gezi Park, and momentarily overwhelmed the police. The next morning, the police attacked again, bombarding the square with water cannons and drowning it in tear gas. Thousands more protesters arrived in response, with large solidarity protests (likewise brutally repressed) staged in most major cities in Turkey. By the time the protests ended in late August, there were eight dead (six civilians and two police), 8,163 injured and 5,300 arrested. Some 845 journalists lost their jobs for reporting on the protests, and thirty-eight were taken into police custody (Yaman 2013).

The Gezi Park protests were not only the largest and most violently repressed in recent Turkish history, they were also the most heterogeneous, comprised of individuals and social, political, and ethnic groups that would not have otherwise shared a political platform. Indeed, most protesters emphatically rejected the secular-religious, modern-traditional and conservative-liberal dichotomies through which the government and some national and international media initially framed the protests. The 2014 Gezi Report released by KONDA Research and Consultancy (2014) (one of Turkey's largest independent public opinion and consultancy firms) offers important insights into both the composition of the protests, and the factors that motivated protesters, including many who had never participated in a protest before, to come out onto the streets.

The Gezi Report confirms that a large percentage of protesters were motivated by a combination of indignation at Erdoğan's statements and attitude towards the original occupation of Gezi Park (30.3 per cent) and the brutal and disproportionate police response that followed (49.1 per cent). Some 58.1 per cent were also motivated by increasing restrictions on freedom and 37.2 per cent came out to express general displeasure with the AKP government and its policies. It should be noted, however, that even though a large percentage of the protesters were voicing their dissent with AKP's policies, they did not overwhelmingly represent one political party. Supporters of CHP (the Kemalist Republican People's Party), MHP (the nationalist Nationalist Action Party) and HDP (the left People's Democracy Party, supported by a large section of the Kurdish population but also other 'leftist' and environmentalist groups) and various other smaller parties were all present in the park. What is more, and more importantly, support for the said parties was not visibly expressed during the protests, with political and party banners conspicuously absent from the park.

When asked to choose a single response to the question of what they demanded, 34.1 per cent of protesters said freedom, with 18.1 per cent responding that they came to protest violations of human rights and to demand their rights. In other words, over half of the protesters were primarily motivated by the cause of freedom and rights. More importantly from the perspective of this chapter, most of the Gezi Park protesters consciously refused to position themselves on pre-existing social and political spectrums, or to 'choose from' available and legible subject positions as a way of explaining their participation in the protests. 62 per cent of protesters stated that they saw themselves 'as a member of a group subject to human rights violations,' with 25 per cent more saying that they 'sometimes' felt this way. In other words, 87 per cent of respondents identified themselves as having been directly or indirectly subject to human rights violations or unlawful treatment. Even more tellingly, 93.6 per cent identified themselves as 'ordinary citizens' when asked whether 'they came to the park in order to represent an organization or institution'. What makes this more extraordinary, particularly in the context of the sharply polarized Turkish political scene, is that the question was open-ended, meaning that without prompting, close to 95 per cent chose not to identify with any particular party, ideology or movement.

The heterogeneity of the Gezi Park protests is brought into sharp relief by the democracy vigil that followed the attempted coup three years later. The coup attempt took place on 15 July 2016 and has, like the Gezi Park protests, garnered significant international attention. Three main narratives have been offered to account for the events of 15 July (Grabow 2016). The first holds that what took place was an unsuccessful military coup d'état organized by members of the army under the control of the Fethullah Gülen movement, FETÖ,[2] against which the government has, and continues to, defend itself (Erdoğan: Artık 2016). This is the most widely accepted narrative, and represents also the narrative offered by the AKP government and former prime minister, now president, Erdoğan. The second concurs with the first half of

---

2   FETÖ stands for the 'Fethullah Terror Organization', and is the dominant way in which the Fetullah Gülen movement is represented in Turkish media and state discourses following the coup attempt. It is said to be led by Fethullah Gülen, an exiled cleric living in the United States. Gülen is said to have created a 'parallel' or 'deep state' through the infiltration of his followers into state institutions, working to undermine the AKP government eventually orchestrating the coup attempt.

that narrative, but suggests that the government had seen the coup coming and let it unfold so as to quash it and to gain the political capital necessary to purge the judiciary, military and civil service of its detractors once and for all (Erdoğan darbeyi 2016). The third narrative holds that the whole thing was orchestrated by the government and/or president for the reasons enumerated by the second narrative (Fethullah Gülen 2016). From the perspective of Turkish democracy, the 'truth' of the matter is (almost) irrelevant (Grabow 2016). In its aftermath, Erdoğan has consolidated his grip on executive, legislative and judicial power, supported by a state of emergency extended, at the time of writing, to at least October 2017, and by the April 2017 referendum on an executive presidency, the fairness and legitimacy of which have been questioned by both the opposition and international observers.[3] In the eyes of many of his supporters, the attempted coup, irrespective of the causes or actors behind it, has given the president the legitimacy to consolidate power through exceptional measures.

Within two days of the coup attempt, 265 people had died (161 civilians and 104 soldiers) and 1,440 people had been injured. The reaction of Erdoğan's government was swift and unprecedented: 2,839 members of the armed forces, including twenty-nine generals, were taken into custody; 2,745 judges and prosecutors were relieved of their duties (250 were placed in custody) on grounds of being members of terrorist organizations and attempting to overthrow the government; and 8,000 police officers were temporarily relieved of duty, accused of supporting the coup on behalf of the Fethullah Gülen movement. The purge was quickly extended to the Ministry of Education and *Yüksek Öğrenim* (YÖK, 'Higher education council'), with 15,200 staff suspended by the Ministry of Education, four university rectors suspended by YÖK, and 1,577 university deans resigning their posts. Within a week of the attempted coup all academics were temporarily banned from travelling abroad. As of January 2017, 97,679 public sector workers have been fired; 103,850 Turkish citizens have been marked as 'suspect'; 41,326 people have been arrested (with arrest warrants out for another 5,150); 5,000 judges and prosecutors have been suspended; 157 media organizations have been shut down; 121 journalists and 12 members of parliament have been arrested; and 527 corporations (and their assets of circa 12 billion Turkish lira) have been appropriated by the state (Rakamlarla OHAL 2017). The draconian nature of the measures taken by the government has led some to

---

3   Supporters of the presidential system won by a narrow margin of 51 to 49 per cent. For questions regarding the fairness and legitimacy of the referendum, see Al 2017; McIntyre, 2017; Observer Says, 2017.

conclude that even after the most violent military coup in Turkish history (on 12 September 1980), the junta government did not take such drastic action (12 Eylül 2016).

Variations on Democracy: The Earth Iftars and Democracy Vigil

This second part of the chapter foregrounds two performative repertoires that emerged during the Gezi Park protests and in the aftermath of the attempted coup: the communal earth *iftars* first organized during the Gezi Park protests, and the democracy vigil that followed the attempted coup. The earth *iftars* and the democracy vigil, I suggest, highlight what might at first glance seem counterintuitive—namely, that the *iftars*, which draw on a 'religious', 'Muslim' ritual, offer a more radically open and inclusive articulation of democracy than the vigil avowedly staged in opposition to the coup d'état and in defence of democracy. In doing so, they not only disclose two distinct and irreconcilable interpretations of democracy, but also the radically democratic potential of the Gezi Park protests and the absence of such potential in the government and its supporters' version of democracy.

The earth *iftars* were first organized in July 2013 at the height of the Gezi Park protests.[4] A communal meal was set up on Istanbul's İstiklal Street, a long pedestrian thoroughfare that stretches from Taksim Square to the Galata Tower. A long, makeshift table (a row of newspapers laid out on the pavement) was stretched between Gezi Park and Galatasaray High School (about halfway up İstiklal Street). A second table was set in Saraçhane Park in the Fatih district of Istanbul, and a third at the Sarıgazi Cemevi,

---

4   *Iftar* is the evening meal that breaks the daily fast of observant Muslims during the month of Ramadan. Whilst *iftar* practices vary, the communal aspect of the meal and the humble sharing of food with others, including those less fortunate, have traditionally comprised important parts of the ritual. In Turkey, however, lavish *iftars* are also frequently organized by wealthy families, businessmen, and government officials and dignitaries at exclusive restaurants, and recently, at the Presidential Palace in Ankara—in 2015, at an estimated cost of 6 million Turkish lira (AK Saray'ın 2015). The earth *iftars* problematized the excesses and inaccessibility of such *iftars*. Referencing the earth both literally (participants sat and ate on the ground) and figuratively, as that which is common, belongs to, and should be accessible to and shared equally by all, the earth *iftars* intended to performatively expose the hypocrisy and excesses of a government that claimed to be 'of' and 'for' the people.

in solidarity with the Alevi community, a group frequently targeted by the AKP government (ABD Dini 2015; Karaca 2013). The *iftars* were organized by *Anti-Kapitalist Müslümanlar* ('Anti-capitalist Muslims') and *Devrimci Müslümanlar* ('Revolutionary Muslims'), two Muslim organizations critical of Erdoğan and the AKP government, whose members took part in the Gezi Park protests.[5] The spirit of the earth *iftars* is well captured in the slogan used to advertise them:

> No to discrimination, yes to solidarity; No to homogenization, yes to diversity; No to ostentation, yes to modesty; No to drought, yes to fertility; No to accumulation, yes to sharing; An *iftar* with no sponsors, no capital, no flags, no banners....An *iftar* table where believers and non-believers, Turks and Kurds, Alevis and Sunnis, celebrities and ordinary people, in short, everyone, is equal. This is God's table; We invite all Istanbulites to join us. (Bir yanda 2015)

Having joined the July 2013 *iftar*, journalist Burak Kuru described the experience as follows:

> All people there had a true desire to join a meal which they had just passed by before. People realised that being together for this meal felt better than many other things. And not all diners had actually fasted. Some simply chose to eat at *iftar* time and dined together with the others. The people there included just anybody in the street...I'll never forget the hospitality and kindness they offered to passers-by. The people demonstrated they need no mediator to communicate'. (quoted in Taştekin 2013)

For Hadiye Yolcu, who spoke on behalf of the Revolutionary Muslims, the *iftars* were a way of reflecting the spirit of solidarity witnessed in Gezi—a solidarity grounded not in being together with those who are 'like us', but in being together in difference and singularity (Gezi'nin Ramazan'a 2013). The Gezi Park protests, and the earth *iftars* in particular, did not aim to represent

---

5   Anti-Capitalist Muslims is a group founded in 2012 with the motto 'For a world without borders, classes, exploitation, wars'. Guided by the belief that authentic Islam is egalitarian and thus anti-capitalist at its core, the group opposes the capitalist excesses of the AKP government. Revolutionary Muslims is a group founded in 2010 with the motto 'Rebellion and Islam'. They derive their anti-capitalist stance from the belief that all property belongs to God and believe in an egalitarian 'Islam for the oppressed'. Both groups actively and publicly oppose the AKP government and what they see as its self-interested perversion of Islam.

or forge a unity or identity—not even a transient or strategic one. Rather, they enacted, if only momentarily, the possibility of a solidarity and community grounded in radical difference and sustained through non-identity. As I argued elsewhere, without sponsors, banners and flags, open to everyone, believers and non-believers, those who fast during Ramadan and those who do not, the *iftars* instantiated, if only momentarily, what Giorgio Agamben (1993) has termed a "community of singularities" or "whatever beings", joined not by the bonds of common, *ipseic* identities but by a spectral bond that is neither, yet simultaneously, present and absent (Czajka 2017).[6]

The reaction of the government and government-supported media to the earth *iftars* is indicative of the radically unsettling deconstruction of *ipseic* identities that the *iftars* performed. Each year (2013 to the time of writing) the event has been met with heavy riot police presence. The July 2013 *iftar* resulted in a number of arrests and trials (one of which dragged on for two years, though those tried were eventually acquitted) (Söylemez 2015). A columnist in a government-backed newspaper was scandalized by the presence of alcohol at an *iftar* (Taştekin 2013). Others accused the Anti-Capitalist Muslims of 'exploiting Islam', accused participants of mocking Islam, or alternately, praised the AKP for leading the 'hoodlum' who participated in Gezi to religion: "Allah has channelled his good will through the AKP", the columnist opined, "to create a Muslim youth and a celebration of Islam. Even the atheists and Gezicis are celebrating it" (Taştekin 2013).

In subsequent years, whilst the number of earth *iftars* grew, they also became an object of considerable debate. Supporters continued to insist on the performative value of the *iftars*, noting that they "symbolised equality, fraternity, sharing, plentitude, and unity in difference" (Doğan 2013) and revealed that 'there is an Islam beyond AKP's Islam, that is against exploitation of religious beliefs' (#GeziyiUnutma 2014). Supporters argued that the earth *iftars* were the only *iftars* at which 'everyone is indeed welcome', (Taksim'de Yeryüzü 2013) and that other social and political movements should take the earth *iftar* as a model, as 'it is genuine, it is all-encompassing, it belongs to the people, and not the oppressor' (Taraf Yazarı 2013). But the *iftars* continued to be criticized by the government, and eventually also by some self-defined 'leftist', 'socialist' (and otherwise anti-government) voices. Some argued that,

---

6   Derrida renders *ipseity* as self-sameness, as 'the self, the one-self, being properly oneself' (2005: 11), as in "sovereign self-determination, the autonomy of the self, of the *ipse*, namely, of the one-self that gives itself its own law' (2005: 10–11).

It is time to replace the *Yeryuzu Sofralari* (Earth tables) (which prioritise fasting people) with Tolerance/Dialogue tables (which would prioritize non-fasting people and which would bring together believers and non-believers in a more convincing fashion). The Anti-Capitalist Muslims made a great breakthrough. And right on time. We needed that kind of immanent critique of the AKP. Thanks to them, socialists, liberals, and the left came together with Muslim ... [But] today Sunnis are not oppressed at all. On the contrary, it is only the non-Sunni Muslims and non-believers who are repressed. As such, if the real oppressed are non-believers, Muslims, fasting Muslims, should come together with them in Gezi Park and have tolerance lunches, giving out a message of co-existence. (Yılmaz 2016)

Others criticized Ihsan Eliaçık, spokesperson for the Anti-Capitalist Muslims, arguing that,

Eliaçık and his movement lie to people by saying that they cherish difference...When criticised for accommodating a beer drinker at the [*iftar*] table, Eliaçık said: 'Those of you who are fixated on the one man drinking beer instead of tens of thousands of protesters, I tell you: We are able to bring him to the *iftar* table, you can convince him to quit drinking.' [This statement] shows that although he accepted everyone as they are, he wants to change them. They can sit at the table as different beings, but they should get up from it identical to Eliaçık. (İyiekici 2013)

The statement attributed to Eliaçık notwithstanding,[7] detractors on both sides, I suggest, are missing the performative force of the earth *iftars*, which revealed (if only ephemerally) the possibility that a democracy-grounding community could indeed be established on the basis of what Jacques Derrida has called *différance*—essential difference and deferral of identity, or in other words, non-identity, or something close to Agamben's community of singularities. Taking for granted that existing, *ipseic* identities were the only possible grounding of community, and indeed democracy, detractors on both sides thus failed to recognise the possibility of (an)other, more radically inclusive democracy performed through the *iftars*—more radically inclusive precisely because it deconstructed the inclusion-exclusion dichotomy through a deconstruction of identity.

7   Whilst this statement is attributed to Eliaçık, it should be the noted that so is the following one: 'They are asking us how we can sit at *iftar* with drunkards. Being drunk is not a problem as long as you are not a murderer, a backstabber, a tyrant' (Akyol 2016).

A very different, and indeed, antithetical democracy was performed through the democracy vigil that followed the attempted coup on 15 July 2016. Almost immediately after the coup attempt, the president called on the Turkish people to come out (and stay out) on the streets to 'guard democracy' from its detractors. The so-called democracy vigil took place between 16 July and 7 August, with some people staying out on the streets for its entire duration. Excising the Gezi Park protests (and protesters) from collective memory (not to mention all other struggles for democracy over the last ninety or so years), pro-government newspapers opined that the '15th July people's movement against the coup organisers was the first time the people of Turkey have come together to defend themselves against their oppressors since the War of Liberation under the guidance of Mustafa Kemal. And this resistance was also under the guidance of a great leader: Recep Tayyip Erdoğan' (Keser 2016).

The avowedly 'secular' and 'democratic' performance staged in opposition to the attempted coup had a very different tenor to the 'religious' *iftar* that emerged from within the Gezi Park protest. Counterintuitively, the democracy vigil staged 'in defense of democracy', and with the support of a democratically elected government had far less to do with democracy, particularly the kind of democracy staged through the Gezi Park protests and the earth *iftars*. Even a cursory interrogation of the manner in which participants in the democracy vigil construed their participation and defined the democracy they were ostensibly protecting, suggests such interpretation. Instructive in this regard is another KONDA report, *Democracy Watch Research: The Profile of the Squares* (2016), which is particularly revealing when set against the previously discussed Gezi Report. The Democracy Watch report, based on data collected between 9:00 pm and 12:00 am on 26 July, 2017 in Taksim, Kısıklı, and Saraçhane (three of the squares to which people were called to for the democracy vigil), suggests that a very differently motivated segment of the Turkish population took to the streets for the democracy vigil (KONDA Research and Consultancy 2016).

As previously mentioned, Gezi Park participants were predominantly motivated by the causes of 'rights' and 'freedom', came out on to the streets indignant at Erdoğan's increasing arrogance, and primarily self-identified as 'ordinary citizens'. The organizers and participants of the earth *iftars* likewise stressed the difference, and indeed non-identity, that grounded the event. Participants in the democracy vigil, conversely, self-identified primarily through their political party affiliation. An overwhelming 79.5 per cent of those assembled voted for the AKP in previous elections, and 84 per cent said they would likely vote for them in coming elections (KONDA Research and Consultancy 2016). There was comparable homogeneity in regards to religious affiliation: 83 per cent of participants defined themselves as either religious/conservative or traditional/conservative (KONDA Research and Consultancy 2016).

When asked about their motivations, only 27 per cent of participants responded that they had come out to the streets prior to President Erdoğan's call for citizens to flood the streets in defense of democracy, with 73 per cent taking to the street in direct response to that call. Even more tellingly, and in stark contrast to the responses offered by Gezi Park protesters, 35 per cent of participants in the democracy vigil said they came out on to the streets for their 'homeland' (*vatan*) with 10 per cent saying they came out for their 'country' (ülke);[8] 21 per cent said they came out to support the democracy vigil; and 10 per cent because the president called on the people, or to support the president. Interestingly, only 8 per cent indicated that they came out because they opposed the coup. Another 4 per cent said they took to the streets for unity and solidarity; 3 per cent came out 'for the people'; and 3 per cent 'for the state' (KONDA Research and Consultancy 2016).

It is important to note that in both cases—that is, during the Gezi Park protests when protesters identified as 'ordinary citizens' who came out for 'freedom' and 'rights' and during the democracy vigil, when protesters indicated they came out for the 'homeland', 'president' and 'in support of the democracy vigil'—respondents to the surveys answered open-ended questions. Thus, when respondents were identifying themselves using the non-identity of 'ordinary citizens' and articulating their motivations through the indeterminate concept of 'freedom', they were emphasizing quite strongly the inherent difference, deferral, and openness of identity that grounded the Gezi Park protests and earth *iftars*. Conversely, when individual responses during the democracy vigil so readily coalesced around the *ipseic* categories of homeland and party, the possibility of radical democracy grounded in difference and heterogeneity was all but foreclosed. Indeed, an already relatively small percentage of protesters were motivated to take to the streets to oppose the attempted coup (8 per cent) and 'support the democracy vigil' (21 per cent). What is even more telling is that, given the open-ended nature of the questions, this 21 per cent did not identify 'support of democracy' but rather, 'support of the democracy vigil', as their motivation (KONDA Research and Consultancy 2016). And, as previously noted, almost three-quarters came out to the streets in direct response to the call of

---

8   While *vatan* is a symbolically and emotionally loaded concept, ülke is most frequently used as a formal concept, referencing the polity that one belongs to.

the president, their presence in squares grounded primarily on their devotion to Erdoğan and not to democracy.

Indeed, reports of coercion emerged immediately following the start of the vigil. Municipal workers from Ankara reported that they were told they would be fired if they did not attend the democracy vigil, noting that names and photographs of protesters were being collected for that purpose (Zoraki demokrasi 2016). In stark contrast to the Gezi Park protests and earth *iftars*, which participants attended despite the risk of job loss, 'blacklisting', or arrest, the government ensured that a reliable number of people participated in the democracy vigil through a mixture of reward and punishment.

To reinforce the failure of the coup—and thus concomitantly, the triumph of democracy, though the relationship between the two is not as straightforward as the AKP government implies—the democracy vigil was followed by a number of other commemorative events and schemes. Place names were changed to commemorate 15 July as the day on which democracy triumphed in Turkey. *Kızılay* ('Red Crescent') Square in Ankara was renamed the 15 July Red Crescent National Will Square; the *Genelkurmay* ('Chief of staff') Intersection became the Martyrs of 15 July Square; General İrfan Baştuğ Street became the Lieutenant Ömer Halisdemir Street (who died on 15 July); Gülen Street was changed to Güldalı Street (as the former was felt to be too closely associated with Fethullah Gülen, accused of masterminding the coup attempt); Bosphorus Bridge became Martyrs of 15 July Bridge; TRT News Studio became the 15 July Nation Studio; the Istanbul Central Bus Stop became the Istanbul 15 July Democracy Bus Stop; and fifty-three other bus stops in Istanbul were renamed after those who died on 15 July (İsmi Değişen 2016). A 'Democracy and National Unity Day' was also instituted, to be celebrated as a national holiday on 15 July, starting in July 2017.

Instituting the 15 July holiday, Prime Minister Binali Yildirim made the following statement: "It is our democracy holiday…It is our democracy holiday because the people have shown that under no conditions will they ever allow non-democratic forces to take control again" (Başbakan Yıldırım 2016). Given the exclusionary nature of the vigil (many non-AKP supporters were scared to not only join the protests for fear of hostility, but were actually scared to leave their houses) as well as previous references by the president to how 'our' democracy needs to be protected from Gezi Park protesters, the statement is quite problematic.[9] Nationwide, all primary schools

---

9   During the Gezi Park protests, Erdoğan defined 'our democracy' as something that belonged to those who voted for the AKP government, and as something in need of protection from the 'hoodlums' gathered in Gezi Park and at the earth *iftars* (Başbakan'dan Gezi 2013).

were also compelled to devote the first week of school to the 'democracy struggle of 15 July', with children required to memorize poems from a government-prepared collection. Among them, '15 July and the Power of the Nation':

> Around 22:00 on July 15
> On the Bosphorus, a bunch of dogs
> On my tanks, carrying my rifles,
> Shooting my own people.
>
> Then they took over TRT
> Made the anchorwoman read their statements
> My country is about to disappear
> And then the chief calls us to the streets
>
> Oh my beloved leader who is a lover of rights
> How can we resist your call
> When it is about defending the nation
> Can anyone resist the Turks? (15 Temmuz,2016)

Theorizing Democracy with Derrida

Thus far, I have explored two performative repertoires that emerged during the Gezi Park protests and in the aftermath of the attempted coup—the earth *iftars* and the democracy vigil, respectively—and suggested, perhaps counter-intuitively, that the former has much greater democratic potential than the latter. In this last part of the chapter I turn to Derrida's work on deconstruction and democracy, suggesting that the deconstructive framework and Derrida's conception of democracy-to-come offer a way of understanding how the performance of a 'religious' ritual (the earth *iftar*) has greater democratic potential than the avowedly 'secular' democracy vigil explicitly staged 'in defense of democracy'.

For Derrida, deconstruction is a double movement that involves disassembling and reassembling. The disassembling part of the movement, however, does not aim to "reach the bottom, the original ground, the ultimate foundation" that would later serve as the ground from which to reassemble (Derrida 2008: 125). The aim, rather, is the disclosure of *différance* as the originary condition and non-essential essence at work in all identities, concepts, constructs and institutions. In the translator's note to *The Ear of the Other*, Peggy Kamuf (1985) situates *différance* at the intersection of the spatial and temporal sense of the verb *differer*, that is, 'to differ' and 'to defer'. As the standard spelling of the noun *difference* corresponds only to the first sense of the verb (to differ), it proved inadequate for Derrida, who wished to designate both difference and deferral. The 'a' in *différance* is thus meant to convey the coexistence and synchronicity of difference and deferral—deferral "by means of delay, delegation, reprieve, referral, detour, postponement, reserving" (Derrida 1981: 8). *Différance*, then, refers simultaneously to (perpetual) deferral and (immanent or inherent) difference (9).

As such, at the heart of deconstructive thought is the affirmation that all there 'is' is immanent difference, and that immanent or inherent difference is the originary condition. Whilst this originary, immanent difference might be concealed by what purport to be self-identical, *ipseic* identities, concepts and institutions (such as 'the religious', 'the secular', 'the nation', 'the homeland', or 'the Turk', as the aforementioned poem implies), those identities, concepts and institutions do precisely and only that: they conceal existential difference and naturalise what 'is' in fact contingent (that is, always-already or originally conditional, temporary, or deferred). In disassembling that which appears as selfsame and natural, deconstruction reveals the inauthenticity of homogenous institutions, identities, and structures and exposes their 'essential' heterogeneity and contingency. In short, it reveals the originary presence of the *other* within the *self*, or in other words, that "traces of what a totality explicitly excludes are always silently contained within it" (Borradori 2003: 146).

Unearthing difference within that which seems selfsame and deferral (of closure or meaning) within that which seems predetermined is transgressive. In undoing 'the self' by revealing that it is fundamentally shot through with 'the other', deconstruction renders the ontology of 'the self versus the other' or 'us and them' unsustainable. Deconstructive interventions, in other words, "detotalise self-enclosed totalities by placing them face to face with their internal differentiation" or immanent difference (Borradori 2003: 146). They reveal the inherent heterogeneity and impropriety of seemingly homogenous and proper identities, structures and institutions.

Deconstruction, argues Derrida, must not restrict itself to "an analysis of discourses, of philosophical statements or concepts...it has to challenge institutions, social and political structures, the most hardened traditions" (Derrida 1992: 214), and attempt to "intervene responsibly (but not in the sense of a calculated, strategic and controlled intervention) in the *cité*, the *polis* and the world" (Derrida 2002a: 236). In the intervention that deconstruction makes through the disclosure of *différance*, we can begin to discern its critical contribution to theorizing the performative repertoires of the earth *iftars* and democracy vigil. At a very fundamental level, deconstruction challenges the ostensibly essential distinction between 'the religious' and 'the secular', revealing that they are not in fact mutually exclusive. As difference exists not only between but also within self-same identities (and cultures and concepts) that we take for granted, it is impossible to speak of 'the religious' and 'the secular' as self-same cultures, identities or ways of being. Consequently, it is impossible to determine, in advance and as such, whether 'religious' or 'secular' rituals are more conducive to or provide a better resource for democracy. Indeed, no performative repertoire can 'belong' solely to the realm of 'the religious' or 'the secular', the 'democratic' or the 'undemocratic'.

But deconstruction, as Derrida argues, discloses not only immanent or inherent difference in what appears as 'selfsame' or *ipseic*, but also that any closure of meaning (that is, the fixing or naturalization of meaning, the arrival of selfsameness) is likewise always-already deferred. In revealing that meaning is always-already deferred (that is, always-already an object of struggle and inherently open to reinterpretation) deconstruction reveals that there is always a potential for what 'is' to be 'otherwise than it is', allowing us to reinterpret, reimagine, and redesign the world we inhabit. Thus, deconstruction enables us to challenge accepted social, political and cultural truths, and denaturalize and revalue accepted values.

What I suggest in this chapter is that the earth *iftars* enable us to imagine a different, deeper, and more radically open and inclusive democracy than that performed at the democracy vigil. In producing a community joined not by the bonds of *ipseic* identities but by a spectral bond that is neither, yet simultaneously, present and absent, the earth *iftars* disclose the possibility of being and living otherwise, and indeed, of a more radical democracy—one grounded not on a community of sameness, structured through fixed and naturalized identities and subject positions, but a community grounded in difference and the premise that all identity is always-always contingent, ephemeral and deferred. The state, argued Giorgio Agamben (1993: 86), cannot tolerate that "singularities [can] form a community without affirming an identity", and so it attempts to reconstitute community (and indeed, democracy) on the ground of existing, *ipseic* identities. Wherever singularities 'peacefully demonstrate their being in common there will be a Tiananmen, and, sooner or later, the tanks will appear' (Agamben 1993: 86). Thus the AKP government's repressive response to the earth *iftars* and its support of rituals such as the democracy vigil is not that perplexing. What kind of democracy, then, do rituals such as the earth *iftars* support? The *iftars*, I suggest, constitute a resource for the kind of democracy Derrida imagines: democracy as 'democracy-to-come'. Democracy, argues Derrida, is the only political system "in which, in principle, one has or assumes the right to criticize everything publicly" (2005: 86–7), and which demands "exposure to an open-ended future" (Fritsch 2002: 577). Democracy-to-come is fundamentally characterized by *différance*, "by which it defers itself and differs from itself" and in doing so, opens up to the "experience of the alterity of the other, of heterogeneity, of the singular, the not-same, the different, the dissymmetric, the heteronomous" (Derrida 2005: 38). Alluding to the grounding difference that deconstruction reveals in linguistic structures, the 'to-come', writes Derrida in the *Monolingualism of the Other*, "gathers language together … it welcomes it, collects it, not in its identity or its unity, not even in its ipseity, but in the uniqueness or singularity of a gathering together of its difference to itself: in difference *with itself* [avec soi] rather than difference *from itself* [d'avec soi]" (1998: 67–8). As I have argued elsewhere, although Derrida is here referring to language, the gathering of heterogeneity—with(in) itself, within a *non-ipseic* 'self'—also describes the interminable movement of *différance* that constitutes democracy-to-come (Czajka 2017). In being constituted by self-transgression, democracy-to-come constitutes a rupture with existing identities, structures and institutions. For Derrida, democracy-to-come must thus be self-deconstructive; it must be grounded in difference, and in deferring and resisting closure. It must, in other words, be open toward unknown possibilities, and an unknown and unknowable future, always orienting towards something other than 'itself'.

Though such articulation of democracy might seem rather abstract, Derrida argues that his articulation of democracy-to-come is relevant to political practice. It can, as Derrida suggests, "inscribe a performative" (2005: 91). Democracy-to-come, as Derrida writes, "does indeed translate or call for a militant and interminable political critique" (86). In turn, the militant and interminable political critique that democracy-to-come calls for can be performed—including through rituals such as the earth *iftars*, which attempt to unsettle the identities on which existing democracies are grounded and disclose the possibility of their being 'otherwise'. If there is a to-come for democracy, argues Derrida, "it is only on the condition of thinking life otherwise" (Derrida 2005: 33). In its annual iterations, the *iftars*, I would like to think, demonstrate the possibility of being and living otherwise, and thus, are moments that disclose the possibility of democracy-to-come.

The democracy vigil, on the other hand, offers little of that. Though it professed itself to be 'democratic', it grounded itself in fixed and exclusive understandings of democracy and identity. Instead of opening itself up to an unforeseeable other, to 'thinking life otherwise', the vigil traded in exclusionary, *ipseic* tropes of 'homeland', 'nation', 'us' (and 'our' democracy) and 'them'. For the most part, those gathered did not gather to defend or protect democracy, or even to oppose the attempted coup—but to protect 'their' government and 'their' president, and in response to his call. The vigil left no room for self-interrogation or immanent critique—of the authoritarianism of the ostensibly democratic AKP government, or the essential and fixed identities in which it traded. Instead of celebrating singularity and *différance* it constituted itself through their concealment and abjection.

Conclusion

This chapter considered two key moments in recent struggles over Turkish democracy: the Gezi Park protests of 2013 and the attempted coup of 2016. Focussing on two performative repertoires that emerged out of and in response to those moments—the earth *iftars* that originated during the Gezi Park protests, and the democracy vigil in response to the attempted coup—the chapter explored both the competing conceptions of democracy they presented, and their democratic potential. By considering the earth *iftars* and democracy vigil through the lens of Derrida's work on deconstruction and democracy, the chapter suggested that the earth *iftars*, which draw on a 'religious' and 'Muslim' ritual, offer a more radically open articulation of democracy than the vigil explicitly staged in its defence.

References

'#GeziyiUnutma: Gezi Direnişi'nden Neler Öğrendik' (2014), *Direnişteyiz*, 27 May. http://direnisteyiz5.org/hafiza-gezi-direnisinden-neler-ogrendik-ilknur-k/, accessed 25 April 2017.

'12 Eylül'de Bile Böylesi Olmamıştı' (2016), *T24*, 17 August. http://t24.com.tr/haber/12-eylulde-bile-boylesi-olmamisti-develt-memuruna-bu-kadar-zulum-yapar-mi,355416, accessed 25 April 2017.

'15 Temmuz Demokrasi Zaferi ve Şehitleri Anma Şiirleri' (2016), www.ogretmenler.com/haberler/2463-15-temmuz-demokrasi-zaferi-ve-sehitleri-anma-siirleri.html/, accessed 25 April 2017.

'ABD Dini Özgürlükler Raporu'nda Alevilere Ayrımcılık Öne Çıktı' (2015), *Bianet*, 22 October. http://bianet.org/bianet/insan-haklari/168555-abd-dini-ozgurlukler-raporu-nda-alevilere-ayrimcilik-one-cikti, accessed 25 April 2017.

Agamben, Giorgio (1993), *The Coming Community*. Minneapolis: University of Minnesota Press.

'AK Saray'ın 6.5 Milyonluk İftar Masası' (2015), *Radikal*, 23 June.www.radikal. com.tr/turkiye/ak-sarayin-6-5-milyonluk-iftar-masasi-1384107/, accessed 10 August 2017.

Akyol, Kürşat (2016), 'Yeryüzü İftarından Çağrı: Savaşa Karşı, Barış Sofrası'. *Deutsche Welle*, 13 June. www.dw/com.tr/yeryuzu-iftarindan-cagri-savasa-karsi-baris-sofrasi/a-19325820, accessed 25 April 2017.

Al, Serhun (2017), 'The Turkish Referendum is a Victory in Name Only for Erdoğan', *The Guardian*, 17 April.

Bardakçı, Mehmet (2015), 'The Alevi Opening of the AKP Government in Turkey: Walking a Tightrope between Democracy and Identity'. *Turkish Studies*, 16: 349–370. https://doi.org/10.1080/14683849.2015.1050959.

'Başbakan Yıldırım: 15 Temmuz Artık Demokrasimizin Bayramı'. (2016). *Birgün*. https://www.birgun.net/haber/basbakan-yildirim-15-temmuz-artik-demokrasimizin-bayrami-120196, accessed 25 April 2017.

'Başbakan'dan Gezi Parkı Açıklaması' (2013), *Sabah,* 1 June. https://www.sabah. com.tr/gundem/2013/06/01/basbakan-erdogan-konusuyor, accessed 25 April 2017.

Benlisoy, Foti (2013), *Gezi direnişi: Türkiye'nin yeni başlangıcı.* Istanbul: Agora.

'Bir Yanda Saraycı İftarları, Diğer Yanda Yeryüzü Sofraları' (2015), *Demokratik Çerkes Hareketi.* www.demokratikcerkeshaereketi.org/node/653, accessed 25 April 2017.

Borradori, Giovanna (2003), *Philosophy in a Time of Terror: Dialogues with Jügen Habermas and Jacques Derrida.* Chicago: University of Chicago Press. https://doi.org/10.7208/chicago/9780226066653.001.0001.

Czajka, Agnes (2017), *Democracy and Justice: Reading Derrida in Istanbul.* New York: Routledge. https://doi.org/10.4324/9781315693330.

Derrida, Jacques (1981), 'Implications: Interview with Henri Ronse', in *Positions.* Chicago: University of Chicago Press, 1–14.

Derrida, Jacques (1992), 'There is no *one* narcissism (Autobiophotographies); in *Points...Interviews, 1974–1994.* Stanford: Stanford University Press, 195–215.

Derrida, Jacques (1998), *Monolingualism of the other, or, the Prosthesis of Origin.* Stanford: Stanford University Press.

Derrida, Jacques (2002a), 'Force of Law: The "Mystical Foundation of Authority"', in *Acts of Religion.* New York: Routledge, 228–297.

Derrida, Jacques (2002b), *Ethics, Institutions, and the Right to Philosophy.* Lanham, MD: Rowman and Littlefield.

Derrida, Jacques (2005), *Rogues: Two Essays on Reason.* Stanford: Stanford University Press.

Derrida, Jacques (2008), 'Fifty-two Aphorisms for a Foreword', in *Psyche: Inventions of the Other, Volume II.* Stanford: Stanford University Press, 117–26.

Doğan, Sedat (2013), 'Yeryüzü Sofraları Ezilenlerin Sofralarıdır', *İştiraki.* http:// istiraki.blogspot.com.tr/2013/07/yeryuzu-sofralar-ezilenlerin-sofrasdr.html, accessed 25 April 2017.

Erbil, Gamze. (2013), *Gezi günlükleri.* Istanbul: İmge.

'Erdoğan: Artık O Zatı Teslim Edin.' (2016), *Milliyet*, https://www.milliyet.com.tr/gundem/erdogan-artik-o-zati-teslim-edin-2278974, accessed 25 April 2017.

'Erdoğan Darbeyi: 12 Saat Önceden Biliyordu'(2016), *ODA TV*, 24 July. http://odatv.com/erdogan-darbeyi-12-saat-onceden-biliyordu-2407161200.html, accessed 25 April 2017.

'Fethullah Gülen Alman Kanalına Konuştu: Darbeyi Erdoğan Planladı' (2016), *Birgün*, 24 September. https://www.birgun.net/haber/fethullah-gulen-alman-kanalina-konustu-darbeyi-erdogan-planladi-129222, accessed 25 April 2017.

Fritsch, Matthias (2002), 'Derrida's Democracy to Come', *Constellations*, 9 574–597. https://doi.org/10.1111/1467-8675.00304.

'Gezi'nin Ramazan'a Yansıması' (2013), BBC, 9 July. www.bbc.com/turkce/haberler/2013/07/130709_yeryuzu_iftari, accessed 25 April 2017.

Grabow, Tilda (2016), 'The "Pelican Brief", the "Coup", and the Matter of Parliamentary Immunity: The End of the End of Turkish Democracy', *Jadaliyya*, 25 July. http://www.jadaliyya.com/pages/index/24821/the-'pelican-brief'-the-'coup'-and-the-matter-of-p.

Hale, William (2010), 'Nationalism, Democracy and Islam in Turkey: The Unfinished Story', *The Middle East Journal*, 64: 127–133.

Heper, Metin (2010), 'Islamism, Democracy and Liberalism in Turkey: The Case of the AKP', *The Middle East Journal*, 64: 491–492.

'İsmi Değişen Meydanlara Yeni Tabelalar Asıldı' (2016), *HaberTürk*, 17 August. www.haberturk.com/yerel-haberler/haber/92122277-ismi-degisen-meydanlara-yeni-tabelalar-asildi, accessed 25 April 2017.

İyiekici, Burak (2013), 'İhsan Eliaçık, Yeryüzü Sofraları ve Gezi: Bir Muhasebe', *Sol*, 26 July.

Kamuf, Peggy (1985), Translator's note, in Jacques Derrida, *The Ear of the Other: Otobiography, Transference, Translation*. New York: Shocken, xi–xii.

Karaca, Ekin (2013), 'Emniyet'in Gezi Raporu Alevilerin Fişlendiğinin Göstergesi', *Bianet*, 25 November. http://bianet.org/bianet/insan-haklari/151578-emniyet-in-gezi-raporu-alevilerin-fislendiginin-gostergesi, accessed 25 April 2017.

Keser, Gülen (2016), '15 Temmuz 2016 Demokrasi Bayramı', *Indigo*, 7 August. https://indigodergisi.com/2016/08/15-temmuz-2016-demokrasi-bayrami/, accessed 25 April 2017.

KONDA Research and Consultancy (2014), *Gezi Report: Public Perception of the Gezi Protests, Who Were the People at Gezi Park?* Istanbul.

KONDA Research and Consultancy (2016), *Democracy Watch Research: The Profile of the Squares.* Istanbul.

McIntyre, Niamh (2017), 'EU Observer in Turkey Condemns Referendum as Neither Fair Nor Free', *The Independent*, 17 April.

'Ne Yaparsanız Yapın, Biz Karar Verdik' (2013), *Milliyet,* 29 May.

'Observer Says 2.5 Million Turkish Referendum Votes Could Have Been Manipulated' (2017), *Reuters*, 18 April. www.reuters.com/artcile/us-turkey-politics-referendum-observers-idUSKBN17K0JW, accessed 25 April 2017.

'Rakamlarla OHAL'in Bilançosu' (2017), *Demokrat Haber* 19 January. www. demokrathaber.org/siyaset/rakamlarla-ohalin-bilnacosu-h78538.html, accessed 25 April 2017.

Sönmez, Mustafa (2013), *Kent, kapital ve Gezi direnişi*. Istanbul: Nota Bene.

Söylemez, Ayça (2015), 'Gezi İftarı Davası Beraatle Bitti', *Bianet*, 6 May. http:// bianet.org/bianet/insan-haklari/164330-gezi-iftari-davasi-beraatle-bitti, accessed 25 April 2017.

Sözen, Yunus (2014), 'Authoritarianism and Political Crisis', *Perspectives Turkey* 8: 4–7.

'Taksim'de Yeryüzü Sofraları: Allah Bizi Hükümetin Gazabından Korusun, Amin' (2013). *Dağ Medya*, 10 July. https://dagmeday.net/2013/07/10/taksimde-yeryuzu-sofralari-allah-bizi-hukumetin-gazabindan-korusun-amin/, accessed 25 April 2017.

'Taksim Meydanı Yayalaştırma Projesi Kabul Edildi' (2011), *Milliyet*, 16 September.

'Taraf Yazarı "Erdoğan Darbeyi Hakediyor" Yazdı' (2013), *Gazeteciler,* 12 July. www. gazeteciler/com/haber/taraf-yazar-erdoan-darbeyi-hak-ediyor-yazd/225267, accessed 25 April 2017.

Taştekin, Fehim (2013), 'İsyanın İftarcası!' *Al-Monitor*, 14 July. www.al-monitor. com/pulse/tr/originals/2013/07/turkey-gezi-park-protestors-observe-ramadan-if-tars.html, accessed 25 April 2017.

Tuğal, Cihan (2013), *Gezi'nin yükselişi, liberallerin düşüşü*. Istanbul: Agora.

Yaman, Alev (2013), *The Gezi Park Protests: The Impact on Freedom of Expression in Turkey*. London: PEN International.

'Zoraki Demokrasi Nöbeti' (2016), *Sol*, 12 August.

About the Author

Agnes Czajka is senior lecturer in politics and international studies at The Open University, UK. Her research interests include contemporary social and political thought, continental political philosophy, democracy, citizenship, contentious politics, migrant and refugee politics, and European and Mediterranean politics. Her most recent books include *Europe After Derrida: Crisis and Potentiality* (Edinburgh University Press) and *Democracy and Justice: Reading Derrida in Istanbul* (Routledge). She has also written for *Jadaliyya* and *openDemocracy*.

2. A Tale of Two Energies:
The Political Agency of Things

Paul-François Tremlett

Introduction

In this chapter I begin with a specific moment of political protest that took place in London in 2014, organized by a group called Occupy Democracy. The protest was marked by the iconoclastic destruction of protest material culture by 'heritage wardens' and police. My interest is in the political agency of protest things (Winner 1980). In order to understand how these things might—at least at certain sites and on certain occasions—possess political agency, I turn substantially to Emile Durkheim (1915: 1960) and then to Jane Bennett (2010). Both Durkheim and Bennett are interested in energies and things, and their roles in the constitution of the social (see also Rosa, Machlis and Keating 1988). Durkheim's account of totemism (1915: 1960) describes how the release of explosive energies is enabled through ritual assemblies of human bodies and sacred objects, the force of which brings the totemic social into existence. However, it is also a tale of a particular kind of political subject which emerges through the externalization of thoughts, ideas and emotions in material form, as signs, symbols and representations (Durkheim 1960a). By contrast, Bennett's (2010) description of the assemblage and its comparable implication of human and non-human elements in 'living, throbbing confederations' made up of 'energies', 'force[s]', 'pulse[s]' and 'charged parts' (2010: 23–24), conceives of energy and things rather differently.[1] For Bennett, there is no distinction

---

1 If the concept of energy offers one framework for juxtaposing the work of Durkheim and Bennett, biology provides another. In common with Herbert Spencer, Durkheim took the view that the new sciences of biology and sociology were analysing processes that were more than merely similar in kind or lending themselves to metaphorical association: Durkheim's appeals to biology were premised upon the idea of a fundamental comparability of biological and social realms (Durkheim 2014: 34 and 2013: 4). Biology offered a means of imagining society as a kind of

between the human and the nonhuman, and there are no subjects and objects or insides and outsides: rather, there are only hybrid configurations of human and nonhuman elements (Haraway 1991). In what follows, I suggest that these two energies and the ontologies of the social and of the subject they presuppose, have important consequences for contemporary imaginaries of ritual, politics and political agency.

Occupy Democracy

On the afternoon of Friday October 17, 2014, activists gathered in Whitehall, London, for what was planned as a week-long occupation of Parliament Square. A general election was on the horizon (it was held on May 7 the following year) while October 15 was the anniversary of the establishment of the Occupy London camp outside St. Paul's Cathedral in 2011 and indeed the occupation of over nine hundred urban sites in over eighty countries by the wider Occupy movement on the same day. As such, Occupy Democracy can be situated within the recent history of the so-called Global Justice Movement that has sought to contest what many call 'neo-liberalism', a form of capitalism that is characterized, by that movement, in terms of the socialization of risk and the privatization of profit (Mertes 2010: 78).[2] Since

---

bodily or organic structure, subject to dynamic processes of change and transformation. Durkheim imagined a series of stages of development from 'the horde' and 'the clan' through subsequent stages to 'industrial society', characterized by increasing complexity (2014: 138–150). This process, according to Durkheim, was determined by 'the same law that governs biological development' (2014: 149; 2013: 167), and it applied also to the evolution of religion from immersion in the emotional effervescence of ritual in the horde, to the affective individualism of modern society (Fish 2002). From 'protoplasm' (2014: 138), 'the rings of annelida worms' (2014: 139), to 'organs' (2014: 143) and 'embryonic development' (2014: 149), biology furnished Durkheim with a language for imagining 'social evolution' (2014: 148) and for legitimating sociological facts by grounding them in the apparently indisputable rock of nature. Bennett's biologism, by contrast, draws from a very different set of intellectual and cultural resources, and constitutes a refraction of the so-called vitalist tradition through post-structuralist thought, drawing on the 'concepts and claims of Baruch Spinoza, Friedrich Nietzsche, Henry David Thoreau, Charles Darwin, Theodor Adorno, Gilles Deleuze, and the early twentieth-century vitalisms of Bergson and Hans Driesch' (Bennett 2010: viii).

    2   For example, as a result of the financial crisis of 2007–2008, in the United Kingdom and elsewhere banks were bailed out with public money, a move which

the late 1990s, anti-capitalist protests have reflected the emergence of various locally experienced and globally linked struggles against neo-liberal regimes and have become notable for their use of social media 'to build networks to share information, tactics, strategies of opposition, and alternative economic practices' (Mertes 2010: 79). For example, Manuel Castells has characterized the Occupy movement in terms of the emergence of 'hybrid public space made up of digital social networks and of a newly created urban community' (Castells 2012: 45). The movement and the camps it inspired are examples of what can be called post-territorial place-making, that is place-making that transgresses the boundaries and sovereignties of the nation-state (see Chandler 2007) occupying multiple physical and virtual spaces simultaneously (see Bey 2003). Groups such as Occupy Democracy are, according to the parameters of this analytic frame, symptomatic of local and global fractures, on the one hand as state-level sovereignties and territorialities crack and on the other, as neo-liberal regimes constitute new global forms of power and place. Importantly, the Occupy movement was more than just a vehicle for protest: the urban camps it generated can be understood as experiments designed to pilot alternative forms of political decision-making, forms of exchange and social interaction.

The Occupy Democracy protest was organized by veterans of the Occupy London camp seeking not only to mark the third anniversary of the global wave of Occupy protests they had been a part of, but also to try to launch a series of experiments in democracy through the staging of debates with politicians, celebrities, activists, academics, and others about issues such as austerity, fracking, and the future of democracy itself. These debates were characterized by the discussion of perspectives on the economy, the environment and democracy which, at that time, were rarely represented in British mainstream media and political discourse. Nevertheless, they unfolded in a manner familiar to democratic, liberal political traditions: a speaker made an evidence-based argument, and a public had the opportunity to discuss, contest, reject or modify the points made by the speaker. Yet despite the proximity of this notably liberal conception of reason to their political practices, objects were never far away both in terms of the materiality of the protest itself but also in terms of the space in which the protest unfolded and was performed, namely Parliament Square with its iconic architectures and monuments.

---

essentially shifted the risks inherent to certain forms of banking from the banks themselves, to the ordinary taxpayer. The move to socialise financial risk was not matched by any move to socialise banking profits.

Activists had hoped that they would be allowed to stage their protest and the various events they had planned on the grass in the centre of Parliament Square, although they knew that this would bring them into confrontation with the police and heritage wardens. However, they hoped that their explicitly self-declared peaceful and time-limited protest would be allowed to proceed without interference. Activists did spend a few hours on the grass on the Friday night, but by Saturday morning they had been confined to a narrow strip of pavement on the south side of the square and to a narrow, raised grass area running down its eastern side, where they remained—precariously—for six more days.

For the purposes of this chapter, the key event of the protest concerns the actions of police and heritage wardens the following day. At that time, activists were waiting to be joined by what was rumoured at the time to be a sizeable contingent of 'black bloc' anarchists and Kurdish activists who had just participated in a large Trades Union Congress (TUC) march through central London. While the Occupy Democracy protestors waited, the heritage wardens—accompanied by police—circulated the fringes of the protest seizing unguarded placards and banners and destroying them. These actions continued throughout the morning and afternoon, leading later to the destruction of two large 'towers' brought to the Square by activists who had carried them from the TUC demonstration to the Square. These acts of seizure and iconoclastic destruction were justified legally on the basis that while the protestors in Parliament Square had the right to protest, they did not have the right to do so with accompanying forms of material culture such as banners, tents, placards, tarpaulins, camp chairs or specifically, anything that might be viewed as a 'structure'. The police and heritage wardens were enforcing the Police Reform and Social Responsibility Act of 2011 (which had been amended by the Anti-social Behaviour, Crime and Policing Act of 2014). The use of these pieces of legislation in the policing of the Occupy Democracy protest has been well-documented in independent and official media (see Graeber 2014; Perraudin 2014; Ram 2014; Rikki 2014).[3] While it is beyond the scope of this chapter to comment on the legislation itself, it is certainly the case that while the legislation is quite explicit about what it seeks to forbid—activists sustaining protests for long periods using tents and

---

3   Anna Feigenbaum (2014) details a trial around Occupy Fort Meyers in America where the court ruled that while 'fake sleeping' was 'an acceptable mode of communicative protest ... real sleeping was not' (Feigenbaum 2014: 19). The Fort Meyers camp had been established in the city's park. While protest with a tent in the park was legal, actually using the tent for the purposes of sleeping was not.

other structures to protect themselves from the weather—it certainly is not clear that the legislation empowers either police or heritage wardens to seize or destroy placards, banners or towers, none of which would be any use to persons seeking to shield themselves from the wind, the rain, the sun or the snow[4]. In addition, it is worth noting that protest objects and structures are by no means always treated this way: in 2008, English Heritage in tandem with the Peak District National Park commissioned a team of archaeologists to document the Lees Cross and Endcliffe protest camp because of the camp's implication in the history of the landscape that the protestors had sought to preserve from quarrying (see Badcock and Johnston 2009). Moreover, the exhibition 'Disobedient Objects' held at the Victoria and Albert Museum in London, which ran from 26 July 2014 until 1 February 2015, displayed a collection of protest objects at a site more conventionally associated with so-called high art (see Flood and Grindon 2014).[5]

In previous research on Occupy camps in London and Hong Kong (Tremlett 2012; 2016), my work involved discourse analysis of mainstream and independent media sources combined with interviews and workshop-style discussions with activists. Likewise, when I arrived at Parliament Square in the late afternoon of 17 October 2014, I was for the most part focused on what people were saying—for example, in my field notes I quote Russell Brand, who spoke during the afternoon of the 18th alongside Natalie Bennett (the then leader of the Green Party), John McDonnell, and Michael Meacher (both of whom were, at the time, backbench, left-wing Labour MPs: John McDonnell is, at the time of writing, shadow Chancellor, while Michael Meacher sadly passed away on 21 October the following year). Brand said that he had been in Zucotti Park in New York during the Occupy protests of 2011, and claimed that 'politics, economics and spirituality' had come together in the Zucotti camp 'for the first time since the 1960s'. Certainly, one of the areas I have been interested in is conjunctions of religion and politics. But, it was not until sometime later that I realized that neither what people had said, nor the distinctive but already well documented use of horizontal process—or pre-figurative

---

4   See   https://www.gov.uk/government/uploads/system/uploads/attachment_data/file/364469/Parliament_Square_Guidance.pdf.

5   See Soar and Tremlett (2017) for a discussion of the 'Disobedient Objects' exhibition.

6   Activists describe 'pre-figurative politics' as a form of political association, action, or structuring that anticipates the kind of society that they want to create (see Graeber 2013).

politics[6]—by the Occupy Democracy protestors to frame decision-making practices, were as significant as the seizure and iconoclastic destruction of protest objects that occurred by and large at the fringes of the protest.[7] What follows is an attempt to theorise protest things and their iconoclastic destruction in a manner that places their potential for agency, centre stage.

Durkheim, Totemism and the Energies of Things

In *The Elementary Forms of the Religious Life* (1915)—a study of Australian, 'aboriginal' 'totemism' that is usefully read alongside Edward B. Tylor's *Primitive Culture* (Tremlett, Sutherland and Harvey 2017: 2)—Durkheim focuses on ritual and in doing so, develops a highly original and influential theory of religion. According to Durkheim, the 'primary object' of religion is 'not to give man a representation of the world' as Tylor had claimed. Rather, Durkheim frames religion as 'a system of ideas with which the individuals represent to themselves the society of which they are members and the obscure but intimate relations which they have with it' (1915: 225). These 'obscure but intimate relations' are organized symbolically: the totemic rite assembles individuals who come to feel that they are acted upon by some external force. However, this external force is not any religious being or power, but society itself metaphorically represented by the totem, the 'flag' or 'emblem' of the society (1915: 206).

According to Durkheim, 'aboriginal' social life is marked by two distinct phases: in the former, small groups engage in subsistence activities largely independently of one another. In the second phase, these previously dispersed groups concentrate for the purposes of celebrating a religious rite. Durkheim characterizes the first phase of hunting and gathering as of 'mediocre intensity' and as being marked by activities unlikely 'to awaken very lively passions'. Life in the first phase is as such, 'uniform, languishing and dull' (Durkheim 1915: 215). However, once the groups have come together, a transformation occurs:

> The very fact of the concentration acts as an exceptionally powerful stimulant. When they are once come together, a sort of electricity [une sorte d'électricité] is formed by their collecting which quickly transports them to an extraordinary degree of exaltation…The initial impulse thus proceeds, growing as it goes, as an avalanche grows in

---

7   Many of the speeches and discussions were recorded by activists themselves and can be accessed at http://occupydemocracy.org.uk/.

its advance. And as such active passions so free from all control could not fail to burst out…This effervescence often reaches such a point that it causes unheard of actions…This effervescence often reaches such a point that it causes unheard-of actions…They produce such a violent super-excitation [surexcitation] of the whole physical and mental life that it cannot be supported very long: the actor taking the principal part finally falls exhausted [épuisé] on the ground. (Durkheim 1915: 215–216; 1960: 308–310)

For Durkheim this explosive 'effervescence' is the energy and the source of the social. Arguing that 'there can be no society which does not feel the need of upholding and reaffirming at regular intervals the collective sentiments and the collective ideas which make its unity and its personality' (1915: 427), Durkheim goes on to suggest that these periodically organized releases of explosive, ritual energy are also capable of sustaining modern, secular societies: 'Hence come ceremonies', writes Durkheim, 'which do not differ from religious ceremonies, either in their object, the results which they produce, or the processes employed to attain these results' (1915: 427).

Durkheim was well aware of the ambivalence of energy, and its capacity to generate quite different effects to the solidarity-inducing ones he described in the *Elementary Forms*: in *The Division* (2014 [1893]) and *Suicide* (1952 [1897]), *anomie* functioned implosively as disorganization, disaggregation, and disconnection, and as kinds of short circuit or misfire, if you will. Additionally, in the work of the *Collège de Sociologie* (Richman 2003) and perhaps particularly in that of Georges Bataille, Durkheim's conception of explosive effervescence was re-imagined as a transgressive and revolutionary energy:

The College…understood the sacred as the centrifugal force at the centre of any social group and developed a novel notion of [political] activism that entailed the unleashing of this force. Activism then was not simply a matter of forcing political change by practical means, but of playing agent or catalyst in setting loose an unstoppable infection or chain reaction. The College intended to spread a sacred "virus" through the social body that would bring the full explosion of the sacred ever nearer. (Grindon 2007: 97)

The work of Bataille and the *Collège* points to the ambivalent reception of Durkheim's work (Jenks 2003). If the British anthropology of Malinowski, Radcliffe-Brown, and Mary Douglas saw in Durkheim's *oeuvre* the promise of a science of institutions and of cultural systems, others have seen, particularly in the *Elementary Forms*, the transgressive, violent and revolutionary potential of effervescence (see Graeber 2007):

> Structural Durkheimianism highlights the submerged morphological forces, legal constraints, and abstract conscience collective (collective consciousness/conscience) that narrate the *Division of Labor*, the mechanistic interactions and associations that animate *Suicide*, and the functional determinism and epistemological collectivism suggested by *Rules*. The conservative Durkheim talks about stability, legitimacy, democratic law, and social conformity, not only as empirical realities but also as ideals for the construction of a good society. Radical Durkheimianism points to creativity, effervescence, [and] the need to explode routinization via passionate association and transcendent ritual. (Smith and Alexander 2005: 5)

Central to Durkheim's account of totemic ritual and explosive effervescence, is the role of objects. For example, throughout the *Elementary Forms* (1915), he makes a number of references to *churinga*:

> [The *churinga*] are pieces of wood or bits of polished stone, of a great variety of forms, but generally oval or oblong. Each totemic group has a more or less important collection of these. *Upon each of these is engraved a design representing the totem of this same group*. A certain number of the churinga have a hole at one end, through which goes a thread made of human hair or that of an opossum. Those which are made of wood and are pierced in this way serve for exactly the same purposes as those instruments of the cult to which English ethnographers have given the name "bull-roarers". (1915: 119, italics in original)

According to Durkheim, the *churinga* are sacred objects (1915: 120) with a range of powers including the power to heal the sick (121). There are also the *waninga* and *nurtunja*, constructions assembled from various materials that are used 'to mark the central point of the ceremony: it is about them that the dances take place and the rites are performed' (124). All of these objects are sacred, and their sacredness derives from the fact that 'they bear the totemic emblem' (126) and as such, it is precisely through these objects that, according to Durkheim, individuals come to see themselves as members of discrete totemic, social groups. At a minimum, these objects function as visible markers or representations of particular social groups and, as such, they are critical to the constitution of social groups. His analysis of totemism assembles a complex network of bodies and objects, electrified by a massive release of effervescent energy. This explosive force not only

constitutes the social but sustains it and protects it from dissipative disinte-
gration (Parsons 1949; Badia 2016). Objects are central to this process but as
markers rather than as agents: different totemic objects distinguish different
social groups, facilitating the high-level integration of the social body which
in turn is captured by sociological analysis. Durkheim's epistemological and
ontological commitments reproduce the positivist sensibilities of the early
twentieth century: society is rendered 'thing-like' (Bauman 2005: 362) and
as an object which can be studied as any geologist might study a crystal. It
is composed of active human elements (it is their 'surexcitation' that generates the effervescence) and inert material ones, and it is the behaviour and
ideas of the former—imprinted upon the totemic objects—that constitutes
the focus of the social scientist.

Durkheim's account of totemism as an energetic concatenation of bodies
and objects does not only narrate the formation of the totemic social: it is
also the story of a specific type of subject, which emerges through creating
external representations, signs and symbols:

> Collective representations originate only when they are embedded in
> material objects, things, or beings of every sort—figures, movements,
> sounds, words, and so on—that symbolize and delineate them in some
> outward appearance. For it is only by expressing their feelings, by
> translating them into signs, by symbolizing them externally, that the
> individual consciousnesses, which are, by nature, closed to each other,
> can feel that they are communicating and are in unison. (Durkheim
> 1960: 335–336)

The totemic subject—if I can call it that—comes to recognize itself
through the material representations it has made. This Hegelian formulation
performs the primacy of spirit or mind over inert matter, securing a particular
ontology for the social and for politics, in which objects and things are little
more than passive vehicles for conveying human meaning. This ontology is
reproduced in contemporary research on social movements. For example,
in 'On the Phenomenology of Giant Puppets: Broken Windows, Imaginary
Jars of Urine, and the Cosmological Role of the Police in American Culture'
(2007), David Graeber approaches anti-capitalist protest as a kind of totemic
rite that assembles human and nonhuman elements, and which is bound up
with the release of powerful energies channelled through both the iconoclastic destruction of protest material culture and the iconoclastic smashing of symbols of capitalism and consumerism. Writing with the 'renegade'
Durkheim of the *Collège*, Graeber focuses on the smashing of giant protest
puppets by police and, working from research conducted over a number

of years at American protests including Seattle (1999), Philadelphia (2000) and Miami (2003), he explores what he calls 'the symbolism of puppets' (2007: 376), noting that they have sometimes been targeted for capture or destruction by police before they even appear on the streets. For example, at the Free Trade Areas of the Americas (FTAA) protests in Miami in 2003, Graeber recounts an eyewitness report which claimed that

> after Police routed protestors from the Seaside Plaza forcing them to abandon their puppets, officers spent the next half hour or so systematically attacking and destroying them [the puppets]: shooting, kicking, and ripping the remains; one even putting a giant puppet in his squad car with the head sticking out and driving so as to smash it against every sign and street post available. (2007: 390)

According to Graeber, a giant puppet—which is made from fragile materials such as *papier mâché* —is, quite intentionally, a 'mockery of the idea of a monument' and of the idea of 'permanence' (2007: 382). The absurd and giant unwieldiness of the puppets, according to Graeber, conjures the imaginary of the festival and the Dionysian rite, and augurs 'the recuperation of the sacred and unalienated experience in the collective festival' (2007: 396; see also Krøijer 2015), mediating rite-like releases of powerful, Durkheimian energy: if ritual constitutes the totemic social through releases of powerful sacred energy, protest likewise offers the possibility of igniting the social against the suffocating forces of capital and the state:

> This, I think, makes it easier to see why giant puppets, that are so extraordinarily creative but at the same time so intentionally ephemeral, that make a mockery of the very idea of the eternal verities that monuments are meant to represent, can so easily become the symbol of this attempt to seize the power of social creativity, the power to recreate and redefine institutions. Why, as a result, they can end up standing in for everything—the new forms of organization, the emphasis on democratic process—that standard media portrayals of the movement make disappear. They embody the permanence of revolution. From the perspective of the "forces of order," this is precisely what makes them both ridiculous and demonic. From the perspective of many anarchists, this is precisely what makes them both ridiculous and divine. (Graeber 2007: 408)

If Graeber's account of violence against objects is correct, the iconoclasms in Miami in 2003 and in London in 2014 were attempts to destroy the representations of creativity and imagination that had been materialized by the protestors. What the protestors saw in their assembly and in their material culture was, according to Graeber, the 'eruption of the sacred through a re-creation of the popular festival' (2007: 396). The police by contrast, saw something else entirely. The destruction of the puppets by police in Miami was, according to Graeber, part of a 'calculated campaign of symbolic warfare' intended to prevent the ideas represented by the puppets from spreading to and infecting, the wider social body (396). If Graeber's Durkheimian account is correct, then, the iconoclasm at the Occupy Democracy protest can be conceived of as the destruction, by police and heritage wardens, of potentially dangerous material symbols that threatened the monumental symbolism of the protest site, Parliament Square.[8] However, in my view this is only a partial explanation for the iconoclasm: the protest things were destroyed not only for what they represented or symbolized, but also for what they might do.

The Quivering Assemblage

Jane Bennett's *Vibrant Matter: A Political Ecology of Things* (2010) constitutes an attempt to explore the constitution of the political—including the constitution of publics and of agency—in unequivocally provocative, materialist terms:

> For some time political theory has acknowledged that materiality matters. But this materiality most often refers to human social structures or to the human meanings "embodied" in them and other objects. Because politics is itself often construed as an exclusively human domain, what

8   It is worth noting that that the Palace of Westminster and the surrounding buildings were recognized by UNESCO as a World Heritage Site in 1987, although Parliament Square falls outside the boundary of the site. Nevertheless, Heritage Wardens patrol the square. Heritage, of course, refers to sites or objects that are regarded as special in some way by national and/or transnational bodies and groups. The institutionalization of a uniformed corps known as Heritage Wardens who work in Parliament Square and who are trained in security rather than say, archaeology or museum studies, assumes that, in Parliament Square, heritage exists as a fixed and already determined quantity. It also implicates a number of specific streets, spaces, buildings and monuments in a British heritage and political imaginary. Following Harrison (2013), heritage may be tangible—for example, it can be thought of in terms of specific materials—but it may equally be intangible and relational. This implies that protestors and protest things are no more nor less heritage than anything else in Parliament Square.

registers on it is a set of material constraints on or a context for human action. Dogged resistance to anthropocentrism is perhaps the main difference between the vital materialism I pursue and this kind of historical materialism. I will emphasize, even overemphasize, the agentic contributions of nonhuman forces (operating in nature, in the human body, and in human artefacts) in an attempt to counter the narcissistic reflex of human language and thought. We need to cultivate a bit of anthropomorphism—the idea that human agency has some echoes in nonhuman nature—to counter the narcissism of humans in charge of the world. (Bennett 2010: xvi)

Where the Durkheimian social is charged by explosive releases of energy that must be ritually re-ignited to ensure that the charge is never exhausted, Bennett writes of a 'quivering protoblob of creative élan' (2010: 61), a gentler energy that is ever trembling but not actually dangerous to life and limb. Drawing upon vitalist ideas of self-organizing matter that is always already animate, Bennett traces the genealogy of her vitalism through Spinoza, Henri Bergson, Hans Driesch, Gilles Deleuze, and Felix Guattari and, using the idea of the assemblage—of 'living, throbbing confederations' made up of 'energies', 'force[s]', 'pulse[s]' and 'charged parts' (2010: 23–24)—she pictures the political as an 'interstitial field of non-personal, ahuman forces, flows, tendencies, and trajectories' (2010: 61) and as an ontological field without any unequivocal demarcations between human, animal, vegetable, or mineral:

> *All* forces and flows (materialities) are or can become lively, affective, signaling. And so an affective, speaking human body is not *radically* different from the affective, signaling nonhumans with which it coexists, hosts, enjoys, serves, consumes, produces, and competes. (2010: 117, italics in original)

The concept of the assemblage allows Bennett to re-think liberal political conceptions of publics and agency, where the agentive, intentional, meaning-endowing human subject is thoroughly de-centred, such that publics can include nonhuman elements and nonhuman entities can have agency. Using the example of a blackout, Bennett moves towards what she calls a 'congregational understanding of agency' and then 'a theory of *distributive* agency' (2010: 20–21; italics in original) in which agency is configured as 'something distributed along a continuum' and which 'extrudes from multiple sites' (2010: 28). It follows that if human agency is always also the agency of non-humans—of 'edibles, commodities, storms, [and] metals' (2010: viii)—then the 'appropriate unit of analysis for democratic theory is neither the individual human nor an exclusively human collective but the (ontologically heterogeneous) 'public' coalescing around a problem' (2010: 108).

The opening question of Anna Feigenbaum's essay 'Resistant Matters: Tents, Tear Gas and the 'Other Media' of Occupy' is, 'Can a protest camp speak?' (2014: 15). Feigenbaum takes Bennett's assemblage as a key point of departure, suggesting that objects are not simply signs, referents, or icons exchanged by human actors symbolising human thoughts and emotions. Rather, Feigenbaum argues that protest things and objects constitute 'intended and unintended elements of communication systems' that 'mediate and articulate politics' (2014: 16). For Feigenbaum, the focus on material culture does not reduce protest things to representations of human thoughts but re-cognizes them as elements of 'broader systems or assemblages' (16). She argues that 'object-oriented approaches' (22) can help direct attention to the importance of physical objects and structures in politics, helping to de-centre human actors from the analysis of politics and political communication. Once that move has been made—once it starts to become possible to conceive of things as active rather than as passive or inert—it becomes possible to approach their implication in the formation of the social and the subject, and to begin to think of the kinds of sites and occasions at which protest things might exercise political agency.

This approach to protest material culture and the agency of things is an element of a wider project to radically de-centre the white and gendered knowing subject, a project set in motion by certain conjunctions of post-colonial, feminist, and post-structuralist thought. For example, in a now-classic essay Donna Haraway claimed that 'we' are 'cyborgs' and 'hybrids of machine and organism' (1991: 150), such that 'the dichotomies between mind and body, animal and human, organism and machine, public and private, nature and culture, men and women, primitive and civilized are all in question' (1991: 163). As such, what Haraway called 'cyborg writing' and 'cyborg politics' (1991: 175–176) point to moments or occasions where political agency is distributed among humans and objects, as one kind of site for fabricating new experiences of the subject and the social. If (Durkheimian) ritual has been a means for constituting a certain kind of social formation and (political) subject, then perhaps the idea of protest as a 'singularity' where the 'critical dimensions of socio-cultural existence reveal new potentials of the ongoing formation of socio-cultural realities' (Kapferer 2015: 2). In this view, the social is less a totality or a tightly, structured and determined form that the sociologist can represent, than a 'force' (2) that always exceeds representation, perhaps something like a Deleuzian 'plateau of intensity' (2015: 3), framed by Hardt and Negri as the other of Empire:

> The other head of the imperial eagle is the plural multitude of productive, creative subjectivities of globalization that have learned to sail on this enormous sea. They are in perpetual motion and they form constellations of singularities and events that impose continual global reconfigurations on the system. The perpetual motion can be geographical, but it can refer also to modulations of form and processes of mixture and hybridization. (Hardt and Negri 2000: 60)

As a 'footnote' to my earlier description of the Occupy Democracy protest, it is worth adding that one constituency among the protestors was a group of women who had travelled south, down to London, to participate in the week-long occupation of Parliament Square. They had come from the Barton Moss protest camp near Manchester, where they had been involved in a long-term action against fracking. If this chapter has been about de-centring the human from contemporary imaginaries of politics and political agency, their presence drew into the protest assemblage of human protestors and protest things, a range of geological and other entities from water to shale to gas, with the potential for political agency—a political agency that, in the Anthropocene, needs to be understood more urgently than ever. The iconoclasm at Occupy Democracy was an attempt precisely to disrupt the agency of things and nonhuman political agents, more generally.

Conclusions

In this chapter I began with a specific moment of political protest that took place in London in 2014, organized by a group called Occupy Democracy. The protest was marked by the iconoclastic destruction of protest material culture by heritage wardens and police. My interest was in ritual and the political agency of protest things. In order to understand how these things might—at least at certain sites and on certain occasions—possess political agency, I turned substantially to Emile Durkheim and then to Jane Bennett, as well as works by David Graeber and Anna Feigenbaum, focusing on their imaginaries of energy and the distinctive ontological commitments these imaginaries implied. I suggested that the iconoclasm at Occupy Democracy was not merely about destroying objects as symbols, signs, and representations but also about destroying them as potential, political agents.

References

Badia, Lynn (2016), 'Theorizing the Social: Emile Durkheim's Theory of Force and Energy' in *Cultural Studies* 36: 969–1000.
https://doi.org/10.1080/09502386.2015.1113552.

Bauman, Zygmunt (2005), 'Durkheim's Society Revisited', in Jeffrey C. Alexander and Philip Smith, eds., *The Cambridge Companion to Durkheim*, Cambridge: Cambridge University Press, 360–82.
https://doi.org/10.1017/CCOL9780521806725.014.

Bennett, Jane (2010), *Vibrant Matter: A Political Ecology of Things*, Durham and London: Duke University Press. https://doi.org/10.1215/9780822391623.

Bey, Hakim (2003), *T.A.Z.: The Temporary Autonomous Zone, Ontological Anarchy, Poetic Terrorism*. Brooklyn: Autonomedia.

Castells, Manuel (2012), *Networks of Outrage and Hope: Social Movements in the Internet Age*, Cambridge: Polity.

Chandler, David (2007), 'The Possibilities of Post–Territorial Political Community' in *Area*, 39: 116–19. https://doi.org/10.1111/j.1475–4762.2007.00720d.x.

Deleuze, Gilles, and Felix Guattari (2014), *A Thousand Plateaus: Capitalism and Schizophrenia*, trans. B. Massumi, London: Bloomsbury.

Durkheim, Emile (1915), *The Elementary Forms of the Religious Life*, trans. J. W. Swain. London: Allen and Unwin.

Durkheim, Emile (1952), *Suicide: A Study in Sociology*, trans, J. A. Spaulding and G. Simpson, London: Routledge.

Durkheim, Emile (1960a), 'The Dualism of Human Nature and its Social Conditions' in *Emile Durkheim 1858–1917*, ed., Kurt H. Wolff, trans. C. Blend, Ohio: Ohio State University Press, 325–340.

Durkheim, Emile 1(960b), *Les Formes Elémentaires de la Vie Religieuse: Le Système Totémique en Australie*, Paris: PUF.

Durkheim, Emile (2013). *De la division du travail*. Paris: PUF.
https://doi.org/10.3917/puf.durk.2013.01.

Durkheim, E. (2014), *The Division of Labor in Society*, ed., S. Lukes., trans., W. D. Halls. New York: Free Press.

Feigenbaum, Anna (2014), 'Resistant Matters: Tents, Tear Gas and the 'Other Media' of Occupy' in *Communication and Critical/Cultural Studies*, 11: 15–24.
https://doi.org/10.1080/14791420.2013.828383.

Flood, Catherine, and Grindon, Gavin (2014), *Disobedient Objects*, exhibition catalogue, London: V and A Publishing.

Graeber, David (2007), 'On the Phenomenology of Giant Puppets: Broken Windows, Imaginary Jars of Urine, and the Cosmological Role of the Police in American Culture', in *Possibilities: Essays on Hierarchy, Rebellion and Desire*, Oakland: AK Press, 375–417.

Graeber, David (2013), *The Democracy Project: A History. A Crisis. A Movement*, London: Allen Lane.

Graeber, David. (2014), 'Occupy Democracy is not Considered Newsworthy: It Should Be', *The Guardian*, 27 October.

Grindon, Gavin (2007), 'The Breath of the Possible', in S. Shukaitis and D. Graeber with E. Biddle, eds., *Constituent Imagination: Militant Investigations//Collective Theorization*, Oakland: AK Press, 94–107.

Haraway, Donna 1991, 'A Cyborg Manifesto: Science, Technology, and Socialist–Feminism in the Late Twentieth Century', in *Simians, Cyborgs and Women: The Reinvention of Nature*. London: Free Association Books, 149–81.

Hardt, Michael and Negri, Antonio (2000), *Empire*, Cambridge, Mass.: Harvard University Press. https://doi.org/10.2307/j.ctvjnrw54.

Harrison, Rodney (2013), *Heritage: Critical Approaches*, London: Routledge. https://doi.org/10.4324/9780203108857.

Home Office, (2014), 'Police Reform and Social Responsibility Act 2011 (As Amended by the Antisocial Behaviour, Crime and Policing Act 2014) Guidance on the Provisions Relating to Parliament Square and the Areas Surrounding the Palace of Westminster', https://www.gov.uk/government/uploads/system/uploads/attachment_data/file/364469/Parliament_Square_Guidance.pdf.

Jenks, Chris (2003), *Transgression*, London: Routledge. https://doi.org/10.4324/9780203422861.

Kapferer, Bruce (2015), 'Introduction: In the Event—Toward an Anthropology of Generic Moments', in *In the Event: Toward an Anthropology of Generic Moments*, New York: Berghahn Books, 1–28. https://doi.org/10.2307/j.ctt13wwzdj.3.

Krøijer, S. (2015), 'Figurations of the Future: On the Form and Temporality of Protests among Left Radical Activists in Europe', in Lotte Meinert and Bruce Kapferer, eds., *In the Event: Toward an Anthropology of Generic Moments*, New York: Berghan Books, 139–152. https://doi.org/10.2307/j.ctv6jmw9t.

Mertes, T. 2010, 'Anti–Globalization Movements: From Critiques to Alternatives', in B.S. Turner, ed., *The Routledge International Handbook of Globalization Studies*, London: Routledge, 77–95.

Parsons, Talcott 1949, *The Structure of Social Action: A Study in Social Theory*, New York: The Free Press.

Perraudin, Frances (2014), 'Occupy Protestors Forced to Hand Over Pizza Boxes and Tarpaulin', *The Guardian*, 24 October. https://www.theguardian.com/world/2014/oct/24/occupy-protesters-forced-to-hand-over-pizza-boxes-and-tarpaulin.

Ram, A. (2014), 'Occupy Protestors to Leave London's Parliament Square', *Financial Times*, 26 October.

Richman, Michèle, (2003), 'Myth, Power and the Sacred: Anti–Utilitarianism in the Collège de sociologie 1937–9', *Economy and Society*, 32: 29–47.

Rikki, 2014, 'Occupy Democracy: The Battle of the Tarpaulin', https://www.indymedia.org.uk/en/2014/10/518468.html.

Riley, Alexander T. 2005, ''Renegade Durkheimianism' and the Transgressive Left Sacred', in Jeffrey C. Alexander and Philip Smith, eds., *The Cambridge Companion to Durkheim*, Cambridge: Cambridge University Press, 274–301. https://doi.org/10.1017/CCOL9780521806725.011.

Rosa, Eugene A., Gary E. Machlis, and Kenneth M. Keating 1988, 'Energy and Society' in *Annual Review of Sociology*, 14: 149–172. https://doi.org/10.1146/annurev.so.14.080188.001053.

Soar, Katy, and Paul-François Tremlett (2017), 'Protest Objects: *Bricolage, Performance* and CounterArchaeology', *World Archaeology*, 49: 423–434. https://doi.org/10.1080/00438243.2017.1350600.

Smith, Philip, and Jeffrey C. Alexander (2005), 'Introduction: The New Durkheim'. in *The Cambridge Companion to Durkheim*. Cambridge: Cambridge University Press, 1–37. https://doi.org/10.1017/CCOL9780521806725.001.

Tremlett, Paul-François (2012), 'Occupied Territory at the Interstices of the Sacred: Between Capital and Community', *Religion and Society: Advances in Research*, 3: 130–141. https://doi.org/10.3167/arrs.2012.030108.

Tremlett, Paul-François (2016), 'Affective Dissent in the Heart of the Capitalist Utopia: Occupy Hong Kong and the Sacred', *Sociology*, 50: 1156–1169. https://doi.org/10.1177/0038038515591943.

Tremlett, Paul-François, Liam T. Sutherland, and Graham Harvey, eds. (2017), *Edward Burnett Tylor, Religion and Culture*, London: Bloomsbury.

Tylor, Eward Burnett (1903), *Primitive Culture: Researches into the Development of Mythology, Philosophy, Religion, Language, Art and Custom,* vols. 1–2, 4th ed., London: John Murray.

Winner, Langdon (1980), 'Do Artifacts Have Politics?' *Daedalus*, 109: 121–136.

About the Author

Paul-François Tremlett is a senior lecturer in religious studies at The Open University. He is interested in religions and processes of rapid religious and social change. Publications include *Claude Lévi-Strauss: The Structuring Mind* (Equinox, 2008) as well as the co-edited volumes *Re-Writing Culture in Taiwan* (Routledge 2008) and *Edward Burnett Tylor, Religion and Culture* (Bloomsbury 2017). He is co-editor of the Bloomsbury book series Studies in Religion, Space and Place.

3. Making Ritual Enactments Political: Free Speech after the Charlie Hebdo Attacks

Zaki Nahaboo

Introduction

Since the *Jyllands-Posten* cartoon of Muhammad wearing a bomb for a turban in 2005 there has been a proliferation of images depicting the prophet of Islam. Some have viewed the cartoonists' drawings as championing liberal values and rallying against a perceived climate of political correctness (Fourest 2009; Murray 2015). Others have decried the images as blasphemous, with a few individuals engaging in deadly violence against the offending cartoonists (*Telegraph* 2015). It is against this backdrop that the cartoons of Muhammad have become largely viewed as a litmus test for liberal democracy. Deciding whether to publish the illustrations traverses the familiar junctures of free speech or hate speech, and individual positive liberty or state security (Ash 2016). However, the politics of the cartoon controversy also exceed the arguments made and decisions reached. Drawings of Muhammad and their circulation are performative; the images have come to both symbolise and enact political identifications. The global dissemination of the cartoons generate notions of a permissive, liberal, and democratic West in juxtaposition to repressed, repressive, regressive, and censoring Muslims who fail to abide by the terms of being tolerant subjects (Mondal 2014; Todd 2015). Similarly, Satvinder Juss (2015) noted that the illustrations were not enforcements of liberal neutrality, in regard to critical humour, but rather a way of organising contempt for racialized minorities.

This chapter offers a novel account of the performative effects of the cartoon controversy by revisiting the 2015 'Je suis Charlie' mobilizations in France and effigies of the editor of the French satirical magazine *Charlie Hebdo* in Pakistan. To stage this investigation, I first introduce ritual enactments as a prism for exploring the political dimensions of social movements. I then analyse ritual enactments within the 'Je suis Charlie' movement to reveal how free speech became a practice of image making, which transforms the meaning of free speech beyond its classic liberal problematic. Lastly, a response to this expression of free speech is traced through the destruction of the former editor-in-chief of Charlie Hebdo, Stéphane Charbonnier, in effigy. This iconoclasm is shown to expose the reification of free speech in aspects of the 'Je suis Charlie' movement, while unintentionally producing materialist and spatial engagements with free speech. The prism of ritual enactments enables a new vantage point for exploring 'what is done to free speech' in the cartoon controversy.

What Ritual Enactments Do

Rituals can be described as repetitive rule-bound actions that involve pre-scribed and evocative representational practices, which create, galvanise, transmit, reflect, or disrupt norms and values (Moore and Myerhoff 1977: 7–8). This description does not provide a comprehensive or universally agreed list of rituals' features. Instead it indicates typical ways of doing ritu-alization. This is a process of making a set of actions travel from one context into another, with transposition and re-signification becoming deemed ritu-alistic only in contradistinction to other ways of acting, often by techniques of 'formalization' and 'periodization' (Bell, cited in Hollywood 2002: 112). Since definitions of what constitutes ritual are therefore context-dependent and contingent, I find a more productive line of inquiry into the topic would be to explore what is achieved, and can be brought into view when subject-ing social activity to ritualization. The features of rituals I have outlined circulate to legitimate democratic institutions and enact protest.

On the one hand, rituals are seen as having a symbolic function for inte-grating subjects into shared meanings of democracy. Ceremonial events transform actions, bodies, and objects into stylized symbols and expres-sions of sovereignty that regulate the form and site of legitimate democratic authority (Lukes 1975; Waylen 2010; Bryne 2014; Johnson et al. 2014). These processes of ritualization also facilitate the orderly running of every-day political business through parliamentary debates (Lovenduski 2014), electioneering (Brewin 2008; Lawrence 2011), and public consultation meetings (McComas et al. 2010).

On the other hand, ritualized actions can produce disruptive political effects. Mario Diani and Donatella della Porta (2006: 110) note that 'all pro-test events promoted by [social] movements have a ritual dimension'. Protest rituals involve 'dramatic' or 'spectacular' marshalled displays, such as act-ing out the consequences of a political issue, stylized collective recounting of injustices (Della Porta and Diani 2006: 110), repetitive iconic imagery, and scripted chanting. These repertoires of action can be interpreted through a register of 'political contention' (Tilly 2006: 20) since they involve publicly orchestrated action that places demands upon another party, while locating the state acting either as target of protest or broker of conflicting interests. Ritualized activity in protest events can also do more than express intentional goal-orientated activity that aims to induce change in a wider public. Protest rituals 'call to order' a protest community; they cultivate affective bonds that sustain protest and shape collective identifications (Crossley 2004: 49).

Classical social movement theory has illuminated the conditions that facilitate politically subversive rituals (Pfaff and Yang 2001), as well as examined the efficacy of ritualistic displays beyond the protest event by assessing its impact upon government policy (Chvasta 2006). Yet we still lack an analytical understanding of instances where protest rituals become a constitutive moment of the political. To work towards redressing this omission, facets of 'enacting citizenship' (Isin 2012:108–148) and 'ritual enactments' (Grimes 2014: 243–246) can be drawn upon.

One way of approaching the political is to view it as a moment that creatively 'interrupts a society that imagines itself as based on a firm and stable ground' (Marchart 2007, 58). When considered along these lines, the political emerges as a transgression of the policed avenues of deliberation over public interest, making rights claims, and being counted as subjects of a polity (Nyers 2006; Rancière 2010). For instance, the unauthorized presence of non-citizens protesting in public, enacting the right to be counted as a member of the public, (unintentionally) disrupts a nexus of citizenship-territory that preconditions contemporary rights to protest (Isin 2012). Enacting citizenship need not only transpire through unauthorized rights claims. For example, when citizens and non-citizens enact 'sanctuary practices' for refugees (at times endorsed by the state) they introduce international citizenship as solidarity across borders (Isin 2017: 195–196). These struggles to transform rights to reside intensify a contradictory state sovereignty, which is shown to not fully express the borders of citizenship through territorialized divisions of a nation-state and elsewhere (Isin 2017: 195–196). Therefore, the political efficacy of enacting citizenship is also traceable to events that introduce novel meanings to a right, which rupture its established expression.

The actions that travel under the heading of 'ritual' have connotations of 'habitus' and predictability that appear to preclude acts of citizenship (Isin 2012: 110). Even if protest rituals transgress the boundaries of acceptable dissent set by a state, such actions of challenging or enacting a particular right do not necessarily transform the meaning of the right in question. A starting point for uncovering these transformations can involve approaching rituals via their enactments.

A ritual is 'enacted' (Grimes 2014: 196) since it 'puts something into force, exerts influence, or has an effect beyond itself' (246). In other words, 'rituals are performative—their meanings are not primarily constative but generated by the action itself' (Hollywood 2002: 108). This suggests that ritual enactments parallel 'illocutionary' speech acts wherein an effect is produced in the very act of speaking (Butler 1997: 17). Tracing the performativity of rituals also involves noting where its effects are not immanent. Rituals can gather 'perlocutionary' force (Butler 1997: 17) since they have unforeseen consequences that extend beyond the initial event, for example through subsequent media and political responses to a ritual. One cannot, therefore, assume that rituals are always underpinned by pre-ordained criteria of success or predictable epiphenomenal effects, as though they are 'already there waiting for actors to enact it' (Grimes 2014: 200).

Ritual enactments offer a prism for capturing the moment where rituals' illocutionary and perlocutionary force veer from its conventional or anticipated effects. Yet it remains to be seen whether ritual enactments bring into view unique ways of enacting citizenship. This issue can only be persuasively investigated through extensive exemplification and a more sustained theoretical discussion, both of which are beyond the scope of this essay. However, one avenue for interrogation can involve tracing ritual enactments that take place via the collaboration of humans and objects in protest.

Chants, slogans, effigies, scripted bodily movements, and music can each create a ritualistic dimension to social movements. However, classical social movement theory has been satisfied with treating objects in protest (e.g. banners, flags, loudspeakers, photos, costumes and so on) as merely affective vessels charged with symbolic meaning from without and/or instrumental props for meeting an explicit objective (McAdam et al. 2001: 10, 137; Eyerman 2006: 196; Tarrow 2011: 45, 114). This masks how ritual objects potentially enact political interventions. What is not being anticipated here is neither objects as agents, which can conflate intentionality, purposiveness, and causality (the latter extending to all matter) (Hornborg 2016), nor objects as fetishes under a purportedly demystifying anthropological gaze. Instead, assemblages of humans-objects in protest can emerge to shape protest rituals as disruptive events. For instance, the 2011 Occupy protest under the HSBC building in Hong Kong demonstrated how agency evades a singular point of origin as it emerged in the networked physical make-up of the protest camp. Shared tents, communal eating, the simple act of sitting, and social activities coextensively shaped the camp as a protest assemblage, marking it as the 'beginning and the end of protest' (Tremlett 2016: 1160). This 'ritual event' transformed a privatized location of finance into communal and 'carnivalesque' living (Tremlett 2016: 1164–1165). Occupy Hong Kong arguably testifies to one way that ritual enactments make visible enactments of citizenship. Drawing from this study, assemblages of humans-objects in protest can be important sites for exploring further how ritual enactments are creative political moments.

The largely schematic account of enacting citizenship and ritual enactments presented thus far can make visible instances where prescribed avenues of expressing a particular right are transformed. Over the course of this essay, I bring these two frameworks into dialogue to uncover how humans-objects in protest rituals transform dominant understandings of engaging the right to free speech. This is exemplified by first tracing the ritualization of free speech through the public defence of *Charlie Hebdo*. I then outline the manner by which this expression of free speech is subverted through the interaction between humans and effigies in protest.

Authorizing Free Speech

For several years, *Charlie Hebdo* represented Muhammad as a terrorist, corporeal punisher, critic of Muslims, and harmless imbecile. The staff were subjected to more than idle threats and intimidation for their caricatures. *Charlie Hebdo's* Paris office received a devastating firebomb on 2 November 2011 (*Le Figaro* 2011). On 7 January 2015, Said and Chérif Kouachi stormed the office and murdered twelve individuals. Amongst the dead were eight journalists and cartoonists (BBC, 2015a). In the wake of the massacre, mainstream editorials reflected on *Charlie Hebdo's* mission as an example of journalism's commitment to free speech (Kote 2015; *Telegraph* 2015; *Guardian* 2015; *Washington Post* 2015). The most detailed rationale for the cartoons can be found in Stéphane Charbonnier's posthumous 'Open Letter on Blasphemy, Islamophobia, and the True Enemies of Free Speech'. The original French title is more acerbic and descriptive of the pamphlet's argument: 'Lettre aux Escrocs de l'islamophobie qui font le jeu de racistes'. The late editor-in-chief for Charlie Hebdo positioned the magazine as courageously rallying against an occasionally censoring French state (Charb 2016). Charbonnier viewed their mission as a challenge to the supposed immunization of Islam from critique in secular Western societies (Charb 2016). Contrary to his opponents, Charbonnier claimed *Charlie Hebdo's* illustrations were not racist. They strove to animate a diversity of

Muslim responses (not only condemnation), thereby further disaggregating a conflation of Muslims, Islam, and Islamism (Charb 2016). One could arguably interpret certain illustrations as furthering this agenda, for example a depiction of Muhammad crying next to the title: "Mahomet débordé par les intégristes" (Santi 2011).

Regardless of the intentions of the cartoonists, the political trajectory of the cartoons has proven to be of greater significance. As indicated through the performativity of the images outlined at the beginning of this essay, the circulation of the cartoons (and impasses encountered) generated fault lines of permissive and prohibitive subjects, which were cast through prior civilizational discourses of 'us' and 'them' (Mondal 2014; Kay 2016). The *Charlie Hebdo* cartoons enabled far right groups (such as the Front National) to align their brand of Muslim stigmatization with its mainstream liberal expression, thereby normalizing Islamophobia beyond traditional conservative constituencies (Mondon and Winter 2017).

As these arguments shape the cartoons as objects of permission or prohibition, such decisions are rationalized through the liberal problematic of free speech. This problematic situates utility, entitlement and equality as criteria to discern what constitutes a legitimate expression of free speech. The most familiar justification for contemporary free speech derives from John Stuart Mill's assertion that the unrestrained circulation of opinion allows truth to flourish by introducing fallibility to existing claims. Even dissenting viewpoints that are wholly disproven or abhorrent function like a 'devil's advocate' (Mill 2003: 91). They allow truth-claims and values to retain their contingent status through debate rather than dogmatic convention (Mill 2003: 91). Whether or not expressions of free speech explicitly strive towards these goals, moral content becomes an insufficient criterion for prohibition; restrictions are only justified if free speech is a precursor to violence (Mill 2003). Utilitarian rationales for free speech view it as a necessary instrument for debating a public good, but one that potentially threatens equal participation in democratic life (Demaske 2010).

Legally disqualifying certain expressions as free speech (e.g. racist material that does not physically prevent participation in public life), in the name of equality or security, is said to transform the meaning of free speech from an inviolable citizen right to an exclusive political agenda (Dworkin 2000). As exemptions to free speech deny equal opportunity to exercise a right, Ronald Dworkin (2000: 367–368) finds the legitimacy of liberal citizenship undermined and challenges to anti-discrimination laws authorized. In contrast, another prominent view demonstrates why hate speech laws do not jeopardize citizen equality or insulate citizens from all forms of offense.

Hate speech laws protect human dignity as a public good (a basis for equal citizenship) by preventing harm to the 'social standing' of the targeted population (Waldron 2012: 118–126).

Liberal political thought provides valuable ethical resources for debating why free speech is essential for democracy and how, or whether, its expression should be policed. Through the utilitarian and deontological perspectives, outlined above, the consequences of free speech assume greater or lesser importance for justifying its regulation. Yet attempts to navigate free speech in terms of whether rights are violated can marginalize inquiry into its operation as a 'ritualized practice' (Butler 1997: 51). An act of free speech repeats authoritative and successful attempts to challenge or injure (Butler 1997: 51). This raises questions of where the responsibility of speech is to be attributed since its force derives from the historicity of the statement, despite its performance always being cast as original by an 'author' (Butler 1997: 50–52). This also means that an act of free speech never reaches a conclusion.

How an act of free speech is iterated through its defence or contestation can achieve more than discrepant responses. It can introduce difference to established meanings of free speech. For the remainder of the essay, ritual enactments are shown to transform the meaning of free speech beyond its liberal expression. This is first illustrated through the 'Je suis Charlie' response to the 7 January 2015 killings, which exemplifies the remaking of free speech as a constitutive moment of a French people.

Shortly after the 7 January 2015 murder of *Charlie Hebdo* staff, Joachim Roncin (artistic director of the magazine *Stylist*) tweeted the words, 'Je suis Charlie'. The phrase went viral and was quickly adopted as a slogan in defiance of the Kouachi brothers' atrocities. Aside from circulating the Internet, the slogan was etched on buildings, pavements, and city maps of Paris (Welch and Perivolaris 2016). The graffiti reflected a conjoined appropriation of public space from the violence of the Kouachi brothers and a trace of anonymous public solidarity (Welch and Perivolaris 2016). Through the 'Je suis Charlie' marches that arose in the wake of the killings, solidarity fleetingly acquired a ritualistic dimension. In London and Paris vigils were held in response to the flashpoint of horrific terrorism (Dearden 2015). In Trafalgar Square pens were laid out to encircle flowers and 'Je suis Charlie' signs (Sumiala 2017: 120). On 11 January 2015 La Place de la République saw an immense gathering around the statue of Marianne, the symbolic embodiment of liberty and the French republic. Candles and condolences were part of the atmosphere of solidarity that extended across the square (Willsher and Quinn 2015).

The 'Je suis Charlie' 'mourning rituals' in public squares (Sumiala 2017: 116–122) carried the slogan's various connotations: identification with the cartoonists' agenda, a defence of free speech in general, opposition to terrorism, and shared vulnerability (Leone 2015). Yet the mourning/protest rituals condensed and prescribed more than symbolic activity. 'Je Suis Charlie' mobilizations enacted free speech as *the* pinnacle and overriding republican value, which in turn operated as a rallying point for national unity (Fassin 2015). Due to a championing of liberty as unfettered free speech, some Muslims in France felt they could not partake in the semi-official national mourning/protest events (Fassin 2015). The congregation around Marianne demonstrated how this stigmatisation was materially generated.

The body of Marianne, as synecdoche of the nation, became a testimony to enduring values of free speech through the ritual mourning/protest. However, in recent years the unveiled portrayal of Marianne has itself become part of her traditional symbolism, thereby casting bodies that do not conform to this image (certain veiled Muslim populations) outside the national imaginary (Hancock 2015). The placing of 'Je suis Charlie' signs at the plinth of the statue transformed free speech into a founding value of the republic and a constitutive moment of national unity, but in doing so it also (unintentionally) curtailed who could authentically embody the French nation.

Mobilizing free speech as a trope for unifying a political community also problematised free speech as traceable to particular authors (symbolic or otherwise).

Like the literal demonstration of the hashtag #JeSuisEnTerrasse after the November 2015 Bataclan attacks, 'Je suis Charlie' physical congregations were responses to heightened anxiety regarding occupation of public space (Browning 2017). The confluence of the 'Je suis Charlie' signs and individuals occupying public squares, reclaiming the streets of Paris from the bloodshed, enacted the right to appear in public that was disassociated from a particular cultural signification. This was possible through the 'Je suis Charlie' mobilization, since the slogan was not only alluding to a prior act or agent of free speech. It also invoked a social imaginary and constituency that is without precedence, only coming into being through its naming and shared vulnerability (Kepel 2015: 173). One further instance of how ritual enactments transformed free speech, without being a constitutive moment of a national people, is through reactions to the perceived iconoclasm of the *Charlie Hebdo* Muhammad cartoons.

Touching Free Speech

Secular iconoclasm involves removing religious practices/objects from public view or transforming their meaning, so they are no longer given the political currency or venerated symbolism they once afforded (Howe 2009). Those who resist this regulation of public space are often consigned as backwards idolaters in contradistinction to the progressive iconoclast: 'until it is shown that [the idolater] can be educated into full humanity, he is a fit object for … exile from the community' (Mitchell, cited in Howe 2009: 650). According to Charbonnier, *Charlie Hebdo's* Muhammad cartoons engaged in secular iconoclasm by rendering Islam comparable to other faiths in regard to public critique (Charb 2016).

The trajectory of the cartoons also paralleled what James Noyes notes as the modernity of iconoclasm through its technical production, whereby 'the processes involved in the destruction of the sacred image or site are the same processes involved in the construction of a model of the state' (Noyes 2013: 182). This becomes apparent when revisiting the statue of Marianne, discussed in the previous section. During this moment of the 'Je suis Charlie' mobilization, a link between iconoclasm and free speech also became cemented to further enact a French people. Stéphane Mahé's iconic photograph of an individual atop of the statue holding a giant pencil came to be labelled 'Le crayon guidant le peuple' in reference to Eugene Delacroix's *'La liberté guidant le peuple'* (Lachasse 2015). Although the photograph can be taken as a more abstract defence of free speech, the comparison of images appropriately binds iconoclasm to the social imaginary of revolutionary France. As Richard Clay (2012) extensively documents, the violence against images and statues associated with the Ancien Régime was part of crafting the Republic, with a French people being enacted through official and popular iconoclasm.

Although the etymology of iconoclasm lends itself to the act of image breaking, such connotations can be misleading since it prevents one from viewing iconoclasm as a creative 'sign transformation' (Clay 2012: 8). Iconoclasm is a 'structure of beliefs about other peoples' beliefs' (Mitchell 2005: 20). The act of destroying supposedly cherished values involves creating and rendering a 'sacred' idea 'profane' (Rambelli and Reinders 2007: 18). The transformation or destruction of an object deemed sacred does not always eradicate the image of the object. An image can gain greater sacristy and life through the destructive act. This became evident through the violence directed at liberal and far-right depicters of Muhammad.

The attacks on *Charlie Hebdo* can be situated within broader violent reactions against those the perpetrators considered blasphemers. An affiliate of

Al Shabab shouted 'revenge' as he attempted to murder the artist responsible for the 2005 *Jyllands-Posten* Muhammad cartoons, Kurt Westergard (Burns 2010).

Omar El-Hussain attempted to kill Lars Vilks, the cartoonist who depicted Muhammad as a dog, in Copenhagen (BBC 2015b). The American Freedom Defense Initiative held a Muhammad art contest in Garland, Texas. Elton Simpson and Nadir Soofi interrupted the event with gunfire, causing no fatalities (BBC 2015c). Each case may appear to highlight violence as responsive to a prior iconoclasm, namely the cartoons. However, the violent actions against the cartoonists are themselves part of what makes the drawings an act of iconoclasm.

Through the cartoons we find the traditional scenario where 'iconoclasm is written into the icon' (Taussig 2015: 154). Yet its taboo demanding 'respect' and 'defacement' is not created by the ardent believer, but instead by the cartoonists (154). Rare images of Muhammad riding the Bouraq to Jerusalem circulated prior to the fifteenth century (Aboudrar 2015) and paintings of Muhammad found in the Ottoman Empire glorified him as a general in the late sixteenth century (Klausen 2009). The iconoclasm of the cartoons did not work upon prior depictions of Muhammad. The caricatures emerged as iconoclasm by relying on notions of Muhammad's sacredness as rooted in an unspecified image, which in turn creates an icon resistant to pictorial representation and demanding of resistance. The January 2015 *Charlie Hebdo* attackers were complicit in this process of idol production and iconoclasm; one of the gunmen proclaimed to 'have avenged the Prophet Muhammad' (Sage 2015).

Not all violent reactions to cartoonists' actions and the 'Je suis Charlie' movement participate in iconoclasm to the same effect. In political protests, animosity towards prominent individuals is sometimes expressed through ridicule, mutilation, hanging, and/or burning in effigy. The use of effigies in protest offers dramatic parody and violence that subverts the positive symbolism attached to events or figures (McAdam et al. 2001: 10). The intended purpose of effigies is to summon individuals, and the political cultures they purportedly represent, to be tried *in absentia*. On 23 January 2015 the trajectory of making *Charlie Hebdo* into an icon of free speech took a distinctive turn as its once prominent cartoonist was personified on Srinagar's streets and burnt in effigy (Rafiq 2015). Stéphane Charbonnier was constructed out of wood, dressed in a shirt, and a red necktie. A photo of the cartoonist was stuck to the effigy's head, with a caption reading: 'Hell With Charlie Hebdo' (Nazir 2015). In that same month, Lahore, Karachi, Islamabad, Quetta, Peshawar, and Multan erupted in protest; cartoonists, the French tricolour, and François Hollande were all burnt in effigy (Agence France-Presse 2015).

Through the protests in Pakistan (and Indian-administered Kashmir) effigies became a substitutive act of violence against those who continue to pictorially represent Muhammad. This reflects a general use of effigies as a 'proxy target', indicating the 'make believe of the protest ritual' (Crossley 2004: 49). Aside from offering a surrogate body, effigies functioned as an incitement to violence upon those who showed solidarity with *Charlie Hebdo*. The hostility formed part of the context of deadly protest and justifications for the *Charlie Hebdo* massacre (Adamou 2015; Marszal 2015). This was epitomized through a protester's slogan 'if you are Charlie then I am Kouchi' (Nazir 2015), in reference to the gunmen. In addition, the Srinagar protest emerged because it was a 'mediatized ritual': the reporting of a ritualised practice does not merely represent or mobilise pre-existing collective actions, it performs ritual publics in the act of representation (Cottle 2006: 415–416). As images of protesters holding signs (written in English) were presented online, the media was not only implicated in shaping their global audience. The dissemination of the protest images circulated the symbolic violence against the 'Je suis Charlie' mobilization.

The Srinagar protest clearly transgressed the liberal terms of practicing free speech by directly courting violence. The effigies were used as a threat to silence opponents. Less apparent is the transformation of free speech through the effigy. Before outlining this alternative, a deeper understanding of how the effigy operated as a ritual object is required. Paul Basu notes the dichotomous ways of perceiving a ritual object's signification (e.g. sacred/profane, death/life) are unravelled through its ontological 'inbetweeness'. A ritual object is always already entangled in a continuous re-contextualization, a process of dissolving and recomposing relationships with other objects and practices, which works to perpetually dislocate its signification from a seemingly originary meaning. This situation of flux can disrupt established expectations of what a ritual object is meant to carry (Basu 2017).

The burning of Charbonnier in effigy indicated a 'movement of images' (Latour, cited in Finnegan and Kang 2004: 395); it resists a singular meaning, bearing more uncertainty than a liberal expression of free speech or its rejection. In the previous section, free speech was shown to emerge as a marker of cultural identification through the assemblage of Marianne and protestors. Burning the effigy unintentionally recreated free speech as a ritual object that can be handled and destroyed. This challenged the ability to constrain free speech into a physically enduring visual artefact and cultural trope, as opposed to dismissing free speech outright. Casting this physical relation between Marianne and the effigy highlights how free speech is not only a verbal, written, drawn, or broadcasted act that is debatable in terms of a right to directly critique or harm. Free speech also materializes as a point of cultural identification, which is valorized or contested through a clash of objects in protest.

Conclusion

This chapter explored the trajectory of ritual enactments in the aftermath of the *Charlie Hebdo* attacks in 2015. It is well established that ritualized action becomes central to politics when claims, demands, decisions, and ideas are condensed into repetitious symbolic displays (verbal or physical), to either legitimate or contest an authority (Kertzer 1988). I outlined how a performative approach to citizenship can inform a political understanding of ritual enactments. This laid a basis for thinking through moments in protest where free speech follows or departs from its expected pathways. Aspects of the 'Je suis Charlie' movement were shown to resonate with a traditional problematic of free speech by conditioning and transforming who counts as the legitimate citizenry. It would be misleading to conclude that the role of ritual in the events surrounding *Charlie Hebdo* simply reoriented free speech towards creating a 'people'. The effigy of Charbonnier exhibited a trajectory of free speech that travelled apart from a pre-existing right that was exercised (e.g. the cartoons) or a signifier for generating collective identifications (e.g. aspects of the 'Je suis Charlie' movement). The effigy helped discern how free speech was transformed into an event that unravels its emergence as a cultural trope. Ritual enactments provide a distinctive, albeit preliminary, vantage point for exploring how free speech becomes materially crafted through protest.

References

Aboudrar, Bruno N. (2015), 'Sans Effigie du Prophète, il ne Peut y Avoir de Caricature', *Libération*. http://www.liberation.fr/societe/2015/01/21/sans-effigie-du-prophete-il-ne-peut-y-avoir-de-caricature_1185678, accessed 6 March 2017.

Adamou, Mahamadou (2015), 'Manifestations contre Charlie Hebdo au Niger: "Plus jamais ça !"', *Le Monde*, http://www.lemonde.fr/afrique/article/2015/01/22/niger-plus-jamais-ca_4561719_3212.html, accessed 26 March 2017.

Agence France-Presse (2015), 'Protest Against Charlie Hebdo Cartoons Continue in all Major Cities', *The Express Tribune*. https://tribune.com.pk/story/823744/protests-against-charlie-hebdo-cartoons-continue-in-all-major-cities/, accessed 14 January 2016.

Ash, Timothy G. (2016), *Free Speech: Ten Principles for a Connected World*, New Haven: Yale University Press.

Basu, Paul (2017), 'The Inbetweenness of Things', in Paul Basu, ed. *The Inbetweenness of Things: Materializing Mediation and Movement between Worlds.* London: Bloomsbury.

BBC News (2015a), 'French Terror Attacks: Victim Obituaries', http://www.bbc.co.uk/news/world-europe-30724678, accessed 3 September 2016.

BBC News (2015b), 'Copenhagen Shootings: Danish Gunman 'had violent past'' http://www.bbc.co.uk/news/world-europe-31480921, accessed 21 July 2016.

BBC News (2015c), 'Profile: Texas Gunmen Elton Simpson and Nadir Soofi.' http://www.bbc.co.uk/news/world-us-canada-32582704, accessed 17 March 2015.

Brewin, Mark W. (2008), *Celebrating Democracy: The Mass-mediated Ritual of Election Day,* New York: Peter Lang.

Browning, Christopher S. (2017), '"Je Suis en Terrasse": Political Violence, Civilizational Politics, and the Everyday Courage to Be'. *Political Psychology* 32 (2): 243–61. https://doi.org/10.1111/pops.12432.

Bryne, Bridget (2014), *Making Citizens: Public Rituals and Personal Journeys to Citizenship,* Basingstoke: Palgrave Macmillan.

Burns, John F. (2010), 'Cartoonist in Denmark Calls Attack "Really Close"', *New York Times,* http://www.nytimes.com/2010/01/03/world/europe/03denmark.html, accessed 3 November 2017.

Butler, Judith (1997), *Excitable Speech: A Politics of the Performative,* London: Routledge.

Charb (2016), *Open Letter: On Blasphemy, Islamophobia, and the True Enemies of Free Expression,* London: Little Brown.

Chvasta, Marcyrose (2006), 'Anger, Irony, and Protest: Confronting the Issue of Efficacy, Again'. *Text and Performance Quarterly*, 26/1: 5–16. https://doi.org/10.1080/10462930500382278.

Clay, Richard (2012), *Iconoclasm in Revolutionary Paris: The Transformation of Signs,* Oxford: Voltaire Foundation.

Cottle, Simon (2006), 'Mediatized Rituals: Beyond Manufacturing Consent'. *Media, Culture & Society*, 28/3: 411–32. https://doi.org/10.1177/0163443706062910.

Crossley, Nick (2004), 'Ritual, Body, technique, and (inter)subjectivity', in Kevin Schilbrack, ed. *Thinking Through Rituals: Philosophical Perspectives*, New York: Routledge.

Dearden, Lizzie (2015), 'Charlie Hebdo Attack: Thousands Join Vigils in Paris, London, Berlin and Around the World', *The Independent*, http://www.independent.co.uk/news/world/europe/charlie-hebdo-attack-thousands-join-vigils-in-paris-london-and-around-the-world-9963618.html, accessed 26 March 2016.

Della Porta, Donatella, and Mario Diani (2006), *Social Movements: An Introduction,* Oxford: Blackwell.

Demaske, Chris (2010), *Modern Power and Free Speech: Contemporary Culture and Issues of Equality*, Plymouth: Lexington Books.

Dworkin, Ronald (2000), *Sovereign Virtue: The Theory and Practice of Equality.* Cambridge: Harvard University Press.

Eyerman, Ron (2006), 'Performing Opposition or, How Social Movements Move', in J. C. Alexander, B. Giesen, and J. L. Mast, eds., *Social Performance: Symbolic Action, Cultural Pragmatics, and Ritual,* Cambridge: Cambridge University Press.

Fassin, Didier (2015), 'In the Name of the Republic: Untimely Meditations on the Aftermath of the Charlie Hebdo Attack', *Anthropology Today* 31/2: 3–7. https://doi.org/10.1111/1467-8322.12162.

Finnegan, Cara A and Kang, Jiyeon (2004) '"Sighting" the public: iconoclasm and public sphere theory', *Quarterly Journal of Speech*, 90/4: 377–402. https://doi.org/10.1080/0033563042000302153.

Fourest, Caroline (2009), *La Dernière Utopie: Menaces sur l'Universalisme,* Paris: Grasset.

Grimes, Ronald L. (2014), *The Craft of Ritual Studies,* Oxford: Oxford University Press. https://doi.org/10.1093/acprof:oso/9780195301427.001.0001.

Guardian. (2015), 'The Guardian View on Charlie Hebdo: Show Solidarity, But In Your Own Voice', https://www.theguardian.com/commentisfree/2015/jan/08/guardian-view-charlie-hebdo-show-solidarity-own-voice, accessed 3 October 2017.

Hancock, Claire (2015) '"The Republic Is Lived with an Uncovered Face" (and a Skirt): (Un)Dressing French Citizens', *Gender, Place & Culture* 22/7: 1023–1040. https://doi.org/10.1080/0966369X.2014.958061.

Hollywood, Amy (2002), 'Performativity, Citationality, Ritualization', *History of Religions,* 42/2: 93–115. https://doi.org/10.1086/463699.

Hornborg, Alf (2016), 'Artifacts have Consequences, Not Agency', *European Journal of Social Theory,* 20/1: 95–110. https://doi.org/10.1177/1368431016640536.

Howe, Nicholas (2009), 'Secular Iconoclasm: Purifying, Privatizing, and Profaning Public Faith', *Social & Cultural Geography*, 10: 639–656. https://doi.org/10.1080/14649360903068092.

Isin, Engin F. (2017), 'Enacting International Citizenship'. *International Political Sociology: Transversal Lines,* London: Routledge.

Isin, Engin F. (2012), *Citizens without Frontiers,* London: Bloomsbury. https://doi.org/10.1068/d19210.

Johnson, Rachel E., Faith Armitage, and Carole Spary (2014), 'Pageantry as Politics: The State Opening of Parliaments in South Africa, India and the UK', in Shirin M. Rai and Rachel E. Johnson, eds., *Democracy in Practice Ceremony and Ritual in Parliament,* Basingstoke: Palgrave. https://doi.org/10.1057/9781137361912_12.

Juss, Satvinder (2015), 'Burqa-bashing and the Charlie Hebdo Cartoons', *King's Law Journal,* 26/1: 27–43. https://doi.org/10.1080/09615768.2015.1035103.

Kay, Jeanne (2016), 'Suis-Je Charlie? A Postcolonial Genealogy of the French Response to the Charlie Hebdo Attack' in Šarūnas Paunksnis, ed. *Dislocating Globality: Deterritorialization, Difference and Resistance*, Brill: Leiden. https://doi.org/10.1163/9789004304055_003.

Kepel, Gilles (2015), *Terror in France: The Rise of Jihad in the West*, Princeton: Princeton University Press.

Kertzer, David I. (1988), *Ritual, Politics, and Power,* New Haven: Yale University Press.

Klausen, Jytte (2009), 'The Danish Cartoons and Modern Iconoclasm in the Cosmopolitan Muslim Diaspora', *Harvard Middle Eastern and Islamic Review*, 8: 86–118.

Kote, Gilles van (2015), 'Le Monde's Editorial : Standing Free, Together', *Le Monde*, http://www.lemonde.fr/societe/article/2015/01/09/le-monde-s-editorial-standing-free-together_4552385_3224.html, accessed 3 October 2017.

Lachasse, Jérôme (2015), 'Qui est Stéphane Mahé, l'Auteur du "Crayon Guidant le Peuple"*? Le Figaro*, http://www.lefigaro.fr/culture/2015/01/13/03004-20150113ARTFIG00081-qui-est-stephane-mahe-l-auteur-du-crayon-guidant-le-peuple.php, accessed 3 November 2017.

Lawrence, Jon (2011), 'The Culture of Elections in Modern Britain', *History*, 96 (324): 459–476. https://doi.org/10.1111/j.1468-229X.2011.00529.x.

Le Figaro. (2011), 'Un Incendie Criminel Ravage le Siège de Charlie Hebdo', http://www.lefigaro.fr/actualite-france/2011/11/02/01016-20111102ARTFIG00304-caricature-de-mahomet-le-siege-de-l-hebdomadaire-satirique-charlie-hebdo-incendie-son-site-pirate.php, accessed 3 October 2017.

Leone, Massimo (2015),'To Be or Not To Be Charlie Hebdo: Ritual Patterns of Opinion Formation in the Social Networks', *Social Semiotics*, 25/5: 1–25. https://doi.org/10.1080/10350330.2014.950008.

Lovenduski, Joni (2014), 'Prime Minister's Questions as Political Ritual at Westminster', in Shirin M. Rai and Rachel E. Johnson, eds., *Democracy in Practice Ceremony and Ritual in Parliament,* Basingstoke: Palgrave McMillan. https://doi.org/10.1057/9781137361912_7.

Lukes, Steven (1975), 'Political Ritual and Social Integration', *Sociology*, 9/2: 289–308. https://doi.org/10.1177/003803857500900205.

McComas, Katherine, John C. Besley and Laura W. Black (2010), 'The Rituals of Public Meetings', *Public Administration Review,* 70.1/: 122–130. www.jstor.org/stable/40469116.

Marchart, Oliver (2007), *Post-Foundational Political Thought: Political Difference in Nancy, Lefort, Badiou and Laclau,* Edinburgh: Edinburgh University Press. https://doi.org/10.3366/edinburgh/9780748624973.001.0001.

Marszal, Andrew (2015), 'Pakistan Charlie Hebdo Protests Turn Violent as Journalist Shot', *The Telegraph*, http://www.telegraph.co.uk/news/worldnews/asia/pakistan/11350186/Pakistan-Charlie-Hebdo-protests-turn-violent-as-journalist-shot.html, accessed 5 March 2017.

McAdam, Doug, Charles Tilly, and Sidney Tarrow (2001), *Dynamics of Contention,* Cambridge: Cambridge University Press. https://doi.org/10.1017/CBO9780511805431.

Mill, John S. (2003) *On Liberty*, New Haven: Yale University Press.

Mitchell, William J.T. (2005), *What Do Pictures Want? The Lives and Loves of Images*, Chicago: Chicago University Press. https://doi.org/10.7208/chicago/9780226245904.001.0001.

Mondal, Anshuman A. (2014), *Islam and Controversy: The Politics of Free Speech After Rushdie,* Basingstoke: Palgrave McMillan.

Mondon, Aurelien and Aaron Winter (2017) 'Charlie Hebdo, Republican Secularism and Islamophobia', in Gavan Titley, Des Freedman, Gholam Khiabany, and Aurelien Mondon, eds., *After Charlie Hebdo: Terror, Racism and Free Speech.* London: Zed Books.

Moore, Sally F., and Barbara G. Myerhoff (1977), 'Introduction: Secular Ritual: Forms and Meaning', in Sally F. Moore and Barbara G. Myerhoff, eds., *Secular Ritual,* Amsterdam: Van Gorcum.

Murray, Douglas (2015), 'Paris Terror Attacks: Europe Must Confront Failed Integration', *The Telegraph,* http://www.telegraph.co.uk/news/worldnews/europe/france/11995709/Douglas-Murray-Europe-must-confront-the-danger-of-mass-immigration.html, accessed 4 March 2017.

Nazir, Yawar (2015), 'Protests Against Caricatures Published Charlie Hebdo Take Place in Kashmir', Getty Images, http://www.gettyimages.co.uk/license/462007788, accessed 4 November 2017.

Noyes, James (2013), *The Politics of Iconoclasm: Religion, Violence and the Culture of Image-Breaking in Christianity and Islam,* London: I.B. Tauris.

Nyers, Peter (2006) 'Taking Rights, Mediating Wrongs: Disagreements over the Political Agency of Non-Status Refugees', in Jeff Huysmans, Andrew Dobson, and Raia Prokhovnik, eds., *The Politics of Protection,* London: Routledge.

Pfaff, Steven and Guobin Yang (2001), 'Double-edged Rituals and the Symbolic Resources of Collective Action: Political Commemorations and the Mobilization of Protest in 1989', *Theory and Society*, 30/4: 539–589. https://doi.org/10.1023/A:1011817231681.

Rafiq, Zahid (2015), 'Shutdown in Valley over Cartoons', *The Hindu,* http://www.thehindu.com/news/national/other-states/shutdown-in-valley-over-charlie-hebdo-cartoons/article6816248.ece, accessed 16 January 2016.

Rambelli, Fabio, and Eric Reinders (2007),'What Does Iconoclasm Create? What Does Preservation Destroy? Reflections on Iconoclasm in East Asia', in Stacy Boldrick and Richard Clay, eds., *Iconoclasm: Contested Objects, Contested Terms.* Aldershot: Ashgate.

Rancière, Jacques (2010), *Dissensus: On Politics and Aesthetics,* London: Continuum.

Santi, Pascale (2011), '"Charlie Hebdo" Publie les Caricatures de Mahomet', *Le Monde,* http://www.lemonde.fr/a-la-une/article/2011/11/03/2006-charlie-hebdo-publie-les-caricatures-de-mahomet_1597782_3208.html, accessed 3 October 2017.

Sage, Adam (2015) '"We have avenged Muhammad. We have killed Charlie Hebdo"', *The Times,* https://www.thetimes.co.uk/article/we-have-avenged-muhammad-we-have-killed-charlie-hebdo-77j0vzh8lcl, accessed 28 December 2017.

Sumiala, Johanna (2017), '"Je suis Charlie" and the Digital Mediascape: The Politics of Death in the Charlie Hebdo Mourning Rituals', *Journal of Ethnology and Folkloristics*, 11/1: 111–126. https://doi.org/10.1515/jef-2017-0007.

Tarrow, Sidney (2011), *Power in Movement: Social Movements and Contentious Politics,* Cambridge: Cambridge University Press.

Taussig, Michael (2015), *The Corn Wolf,* Chicago: University of Chicago Press. https://doi.org/10.7208/chicago/9780226310992.001.0001.

Telegraph, (2015a), 'A Terrible Price for Freedom of Speech', http://www.telegraph.co.uk/news/worldnews/europe/france/11331572/A-terrible-price-for-freedom-of-speech.html, accessed 3 October 2017.

Telegraph. (2015b), 'Prophet Mohammed Cartoons Controversy: Timeline', http://www.telegraph.co.uk/news/worldnews/europe/france/11341599/Prophet-Muhammad-cartoons-controversy-timeline.html, accessed 6 February 2017.

Tilly, Charles (2006), *Regimes and Repertoires,* Chicago: University of Chicago Press. https://doi.org/10.7208/chicago/9780226803531.001.0001.

Todd, Emmanuel (2015), *Who is Charlie?: Xenophobia and the New Middle Class,* Cambridge: Polity Press.

Tremlett, Paul-François (2016), 'Affective Dissent in the Heart of the Capitalist Utopia: Occupy Hong Kong and the Sacred', *Sociology,* 50/6: 1156–1169. https://doi.org/10.1177/0038038515591943.

Washington Post (2015), 'Charlie Hebdo Stands Solidly for Free Expression. The West Must Do No Less', https://www.washingtonpost.com/opinions/charlie-hedbo-stood-solidly-for-free-expression-the-west-must-do-no-less/2015/01/07/40b2a178-9685-11e4-8005-1924ede3e54a_story.html, accessed 3 February 2017.

Waylen, Georgina (2010) 'Researching Ritual and the Symbolic in Parliaments: An Institutionalist Perspective', *The Journal of Legislative Studies,* 16/3: 352–365. https://doi.org/10.1080/13572334.2010.498103.

Welch, Edward, and Perivolaris, John (2016), 'The place of the Republic: Space, Territory and Identity Around and After Charlie Hebdo', *French Cultural Studies,* 27/3: 279–292. https://doi.org/10.1177/0957155816648107.

Willsher, Kim, and Quinn, Ben (2015), 'Solidarity in Grief: Thousands Attend Rallies in Wake of Charlie Hebdo Killings', *The Guardian,* https://www.theguardian.com/world/2015/jan/07/rallies-charlie-hebdo-paris-london-solidarity-grief, accessed 10 October 2017.

About the Author

Zaki Nahaboo is lecturer in sociology at Birmingham City University. His current research interests are in theories of political subjectivity, refugee mobility within the EU, and the historiography of British imperial citizenship. His work has been published in the journals *Citizenship Studies, Ethnic and Racial Studies,* and *Interventions.* He has also written for *Open Democracy.*

Part 2
Publics

4. Affective Communitas and Sacred Geography: Mapping Place and Movement in Norwegian Pilgrimage

Marion Grau

Introduction

> Places, then, are not simply spaces where people feel good when they visit them. Rather, relations with places are initiated as soon as children first hear the narratives.... Through visiting, walking and performing tasks at a locale individuals both take something of the place with them and leave a bit of themselves. In so doing, individuals add their narrative to that of others while refining the deepest levels of their perception. (Legat 2008: 36)

Pilgrimage is a particular mode of moving and narrating across territory, in a dynamic relationship with sedentariness rather than in contrast to it. Human bodies moving across territories attach bodies and narratives to places, remember them, fill them with meaning and mark them with significance. Pilgrimage can be seen as a ritual complex, relating narratives of sacred geography, connecting places where bodies have gathered and dispersed over time. A manifold of geographical locations and interspecies relations enable such movements across space. Through them various notions of identities are being constructed and modes of gathering devised. These identity constructions have political impact in that they shape how pilgrims, hosts, and others relate to landscapes that hold memories of religious and group identity. Pilgrimage gathers a messy sort of narrativity, a cacophony of life stories, where place is an archive of relations, interpretations of sacred and secular events, past and present, of people in linguistic and social bubbles drifting through landscapes variously encountered and experienced. How do these ritual movements intersect with participation in ecological and political networks and how do they contribute to the distribution and sharing of religio-cultural power?

Over the duration of the research project Reassembling Democracy, certain events pointed to a serious decline in social cohesion, a corrosive lack of trust in democratic processes and institutions, right-wing rhetoric, and attempts to undermine democratic institutions. Our common reflection on what holds together the flawed fabric of democratic relations in human lives and how those frayed networks interact with the life-sustaining biological and climatic networks has only increased in relevance. The following reflection shows how certain pilgrimage practices articulate a ritual network that reveals the fabric of place and bodies that can enhance the strength of democratic commitments and relations through rendering the mutual dependence of bodies more visible through pilgrim rituals and narratives.

Pilgrimage, then, is a practice and an occasion through which landscape and identity are reshaped and reimagined in ways that have political implications. Pilgrimage creates the possibility, though not the necessity, for heightened perceptions of affective communities among humans and animals and with landscapes and places. This heightened sense of affective community holds the possibility of inspiring forms of planetary loves that manifest in enhanced action for forms of planetary democracy—that is a greater respect for the lives of other beings and the way they sustain human life, and for some, an enhanced sense of mystery or of the Divine.

Mapping the geo-social transformations of this pilgrimage system, I intend to show how water and land routes of pilgrimage manifest relations of a planetary affective community between humans, animals and landscapes (Moore and Rivera 2011). While democracy in its ancient roots is at best anthropocentric, lending neither vote nor voice to persons other than male, free, citizen agents, a planetary sense of democracy as something involving also the rights and needs of other-than-human creatures imagines a rather different relationality. Concepts of the divine and sacred, concepts of the animal and elemental actors are often excluded and remain difficult to represent other than in how they impact the rights of humans. I attempt to draw the vibrancy of trans-species networks of relationships into the study of pilgrimage to see if the anthropocentric tendencies of pilgrimage studies can be thus counteracted. Lifting up the geographical, ecological, political, and religiosocial changes as enabled by interspecies relations helps to imagine how pilgrimage as a ritual system might help human agents imagine forms of interspecies democracy. This essay then wants to propose an affective ecological epistemology for the purpose of describing both human and other than human aspects of a pilgrimage network.

I begin by introducing the history and geography of St. Olav Ways and then describe the distinct ways in which sea routes and land routes are shaped by and shape interspecies relations of pilgrims and other members of the pilgrimage network (Haraway 2016; Tsing 2015; Kohn 2013).

Norway is a country on the geographical margin of continental Europe. Its history has been shaped to a large extent through its geography, especially its coastal regions, ports, and fjords. Coastal travel was crucial to settlement, trade and power relations, Christianization, Reformation, colonial and missionary travels and, in the twentieth century, oil wealth through the discovery of petroleum in the Atlantic off the Norwegian coast, have constructed Norway's current political and ecological morphology.

The pilgrimage sites of the St. Olav Ways network, many but not all located along the coast of Norway, were abandoned or neglected after the Reformation. Reformation churches, following Luther's suspicion of some of the aspects of pilgrimage, tended to repress and at times outlaw the practice of pilgrimage. After several centuries of dormancy, a trickle of pilgrims began to show up in the mid-twentieth century in Trondheim, the site of Nidaros Cathedral, the putative resting place of St. Olav. Following the resurgence in pilgrimages to Santiago de Compostela, also in the late twentieth century, several locations around Europe have shown something akin to a 'caminofication'.[1] From 2010 onwards we can see evidence of a dynamically developing pilgrimage network throughout Europe. The European Council began to include some pilgrimage routes among a set of around thirty designated 'cultural routes' across Europe.[2] One might thus say that pilgrimage is resurgent in Western Europe. What sets pilgrimage in Scandinavia, and in this case, Norway, apart is the resurgence of pilgrimage in a majority Protestant context, with saints that invoke a Catholic past and practices. This resurgence occurs also at a time when petroleum-driven travel and transformation of landscape and logistics have changed much of Norway, and people, routes and accessibility are significantly transformed by the finding, processing and burning of fossil fuels.

Fossil fuels have rendered Norway, long at the remote margins of the North, a tourist destination. What is more, when it comes to tourists and pilgrims, Norway is both a major 'destination society' (Picard and Di Giovine 2014: 6) with cruise ships thick in harbors from May through October, as well as a society where foreign travel is a prominent practice. Norwegians are above average when it comes to carbon consumption, as petroleum

---

1. This term was used by Marion Bowman to describe the process of pilgrimage systems that experience a resurgence that is influenced in some way by the prior resurgence in Santiago de Compostela in the late twentieth century. Marion Bowman and Tiina Sepp (2019), 'Caminoisation and Cathedrals: Replication, the Heritagisation of Religion, and the Spiritualisation of Heritage'. *Religion*, 49/1, 74–98.

wealth fuels many flights to tourist destinations south and west.[3] On the other hand, parts of Norway resemble an outdoor museum, a 'tourism contact zone', framing the place as one of seemingly pure nature and exotic Viking history (Picard and Di Giovine 2014: 5). Bi-directional travel forms one of the aspects of the networks of pilgrimage in Norway. Heritage and nature tourism to Norway and from Norway to other parts of the world intersect and mutually inform each other.[4]

The increased numbers of pilgrims in Europe and elsewhere coincide with what has been called a new 'age of migration' (Castle, de Haas, Miller 2014), and in the context of shifting religio-cultural identities and social bonds as described by Charles Taylor and others (Taylor 2007; Oviedo, de Courcier, and Farias 2014). The recent resurgence of pilgrimage in Norway occurs within this complex set of dynamics: a changing European sociopolitical landscape and hesitant attempts at transitioning from the regime of 'petromodernity' that helps propel migration to more sustainable fuel economies. These and other challenges to established modes of living engage communities in efforts to remap ethnonational and religio-cultural identities struggling with adjusting to life with disrupted seasons and ecosystems. This chapter considers the rediscovery of pilgrimage in Norway as a set of ritual practices through which these crises are consciously experienced and engaged by participants in the pilgrimage network.

The Pilgrimage Network of the St. Olav Ways in Norway

Pilgrimage occurs at the intersection of paths that are densely regional and local, but always point beyond to another, sacred place. In the case of Norway, this redeveloped pilgrimage network's focal point is Nidaros Cathedral in Trondheim, the putative burial site of Olav Haraldsson (995–1030) who soon after his death became known as St. Olav. The summer season is the main pilgrimage season, marked by the annual liturgical rituals surrounding

2. See https://www.coe.int/en/web/culture-and-heritage/cultural-routes.

3. In 2017, a journalist in *Morgenbladet*, a Norwegian weekly, commented on the fact that Norwegians on average fly four times as much as the average European, a fact that is encouraged by the authorities, despite the fact that Norway was one of the signatories of the UN Paris climate agreement. Emil Flatø, 'Norge Tar Av: En reise til hjertet av den norske flyavhengigheten', *Morgenbladet*, 28 April 2017.

4. Tourism, as Lochtefeld comments, may affect how people think about pilgrimage. In the case of Nidaros, tourism precedes the more recent revival of pilgrimage by far, and the blend already is extant (Lochtefeld 2010: 204).

St. Olav's feast day (Olsok) on the 29th of July. In its present-day manifestation the saint's feast occurs in the context of the *Olavsfestdagene*, a two-week-long festival featuring liturgies, arts, lectures, panel discussions, and concerts showcasing church and popular music.

Historically a local tradition accessible by both water and land, the pilgrimage network to Nidaros did not attract many foreign pilgrims.[5] However, churches dedicated to St. Olav—a widely traveled Viking raider and later king who unified Norway and was a central figure in the Christianization[6] of that region—can be found across the region in Britain, France, what is today Russia, and related places.

In their classic text on pilgrimage, Victor and Edith Turner describe four main types of pilgrimage (archaic, prototypical, medieval, modern) and as at other sites, some of them are layered onto each other in this case (Turner and Turner 1978: 17–19). While in the case of the St. Olav Ways there was no known pre-Christian, archaic pilgrimage, a prototypical pilgrimage (marking a founder figure) sprung up around the site where Olav's body was believed to have been initially buried. It began and developed as a medieval pilgrimage focused around a royal saint and is now being reformulated as a modern pilgrimage.

While the Oslo-Trondheim overland route is being promoted as the dominant route with sufficient signage and hostels, new guidebooks have added other options for pilgrims from further afield, such as the historic route St. Olav took from Sundsvall on the eastern coast of Sweden (Söderlund and Sjöstöm 2016). As with many pilgrimage systems, there is not only one route to be traveled, as St. Olav reentered the territories now known as Norway several times from several directions, partly via water and partly via land. The Norwegian government's efforts to include various pilgrimage sites in Norway under a single umbrella have had the effect of focusing the lion's share of pilgrimage activity under one site, route, and figure. This is partially motivated by economic sustainability, as pilgrimage networks are complex to develop and maintain. Many of the modern European pilgrimage

---

5. Webb writes, 'The peculiarities of the Scandinavian environment restricted the pulling power of even the most famous saints of the region, Olaf and Birgitta. Both drew pilgrims from all over Scandinavia, but although they were undoubtedly more widely known in Europe, there is little evidence, at least from their miracle collections, that they attracted non-Scandinavian pilgrims to their shrines' (Webb 2002: 61).

6. As with other medieval royal saints, the political and religious aims are blended. In Anders Winroth's words, Olav Haraldsson 'built up a religious network that also functioned as a network of political loyalties' (Winroth 2012: 127).

networks have benefited from the support of governments and religious authorities encouraging the practice of pilgrimage.[7]

Historically, St. Olav was portrayed as unifying distant regions and fiefdoms into one kingdom under a Christian king and law, and effectively shaping a network of routes and relations into one dominant 'pilgrimage system' (Turner and Turner 1978: 21). Parts of what today is Sweden were at this point part of this sphere of influence of the kingdom of Norway. This may explain in part the fact that it was Swedish and not Norwegian pilgrims that first returned to Nidaros in the twentieth century. Nidaros Cathedral in Trondheim has emerged as the central focus of what previously may have resembled 'interpenetrating ellipses' of the pilgrimage network (Turner and Turner 1978: 22). So far, this effort has primarily included land routes. But since 2015, coastal pilgrims began to travel the older coastal water routes again. The rediscovery of the sea route in particular has thrown the ease with which the land route has been cast as the dominant access route into relief and raised questions of ecology, infrastructure and transport logistics.

Tracing the Geo-Social Transformations of a Pilgrimage Network: A Method of Empathic Ecological Embodiment

In order to reflect on the more-than-human aspects of this ritual complex, this study uses the term *pilgrimage network,* reflecting the administrative framework employed by state, church, and tourism officials. The construct of the pilgrimage network seeks to name a trans-species network of relations between plants, animals and landscapes, entities that are permeable to each other; the network is composed of landscapes, habitations, sacred sites, and the routes and paths connecting them. Along them, human ritual networks rise and decline over time and space. Some of these are improvised and fluid, others provide firm forms such as marked routes, markers, chapels, churches, liturgies, prayers, festivals, hostels and other places of hospitality, as well as rituals of hospitality and tourism. This means that the pilgrim is only one actor in this complex network. This chapter focuses especially on the ways in which travel by water and by land shift and shape the experience of the route, the landscape, and the body of the pilgrim in Norway.

Most pilgrimage studies focus exclusively on the human aspects of the ritual network. Human bodies move in and with a landscape, shaping relations,

---

7.   A look at the history of Santiago de Compostela confirms this.

narrating and forging pathways and transformations. As with other pilgrims, my own joys, frustrations, boredom and pain around travel and its inevitable smaller and larger gains and losses, have become part of the narrative. This approach has meant becoming part of the pilgrimage network. Pilgrims travel a varied geographical terrain, but also a rocky emotional terrain of physical and emotional experiences that become personal in contrast to a more distance retelling of stereotypical narratives of transformation told by other pilgrims.

In studying this pilgrimage network, I use a mixed methodology *combining historical and textual research* (ritual theory, anthropology, theology, historical accounts of pilgrimage) *with participant observation* (walking, volunteering, forming relationships, attending events, documenting in word and image). Textual study of the historical precedents fills in the background for a comparative approach allowing me to highlight and evaluate particularities about resurgent pilgrimage in a Protestant setting, where pilgrimage practices were dormant for several centuries. A developing library of newer guidebooks opens the various routes of the St. Olav's network up to an increasing number of pilgrims, and thus feeds the desire of pilgrims to know more about history and present of the route.

Through this methodology I attempt to read pilgrimage as facilitating 'multispecies encounters' (Kohn 2013: 134) in which communications by way of various forms of 'trans-species pidgin' can occur (Kohn 2013: 144). This means making visible the ways in which humans are always part of an 'interspecies relationship' with various actors, including some that are sacred. These aspects of pilgrimage are challenging to imagine and represent (Tsing 2015: 144).

To reflect this methodology in writing, this study blends genres: participant observation is interspersed with historical, theoretical, and theological perspectives, thus attempting to show both detail and wider context. The material gathered is heterogeneous, relying on the interdependence of the various techniques and sources, on prioritizing relatively informal and unstructured interaction and engagement from different angles over several years and summer seasons between 2012 and 2017.[8]

A working definition of this pilgrimage network could be: a type of *ritualized (narrated, experienced, and engaged) geography* that interacts with landscape, seasons, climate, religio-cultural memory, and a variety of bodies. A guiding question for this chapter is how the study of pilgrimage as a ritual can grasp the larger than human world involved in it and describe how

---

8. I want to thank to Michael Houseman, Graham Harvey, and Sarah Pike for conversations that helped formulate this method.

pilgrimage in Norway facilitates and manifests religio-cultural as well as ecological relations. Pilgrimage here takes on forms of religious meaning-making well captured by Thomas Tweed's definition of religion as 'confluences of organic-cultural flows that intensify joy and confront suffering by drawing on human and suprahuman forces to make homes and cross boundaries (Tweed 2006: 54).

In addition, pilgrimage is one of those human movements that fits James Clifford's concept of a 'translocal culture' (Tweed 2006: 58), one that is a convergence point between the flows of local and far distance places that aid in confronting suffering and help create narratives of place and identity. Thus, helping to inscribe 'ethnoscapes' through a 'sacroscape'—using Appadurai's terms—this pilgrimage network and its rituals and narratives generate spaces of the sacred and spaces of ethnic and national identity (Tweed 2006: 51). Pilgrimages are bodies crossing and dwelling in landscapes where mutual inscription occurs. Places interact with bodies in ways that compel passages and constrain crossings in particular ways (Tweed 2006: 150). In his study of Indian pilgrimage in the Golden Triangle, John Lochtefeld observes that while every 'pilgrimage has an identity shaped by two important groups of people—residents and visitors', many studies of pilgrimage tend to focus on either the one or the other, but mostly on the visitors (Lochtefeld 2010: 8). Like Lochtefeld, I have attempted to consider 'both pilgrims' and providers' perspectives' where possible (Lochtefeld 2010: 8). But beyond the human bodies are also the other than human bodies, divine and animal, and the landscapes through which pilgrims travel and in which people dwell.

Rituals operate in environments that are simultaneously biological, geographical, social, political, historical, and cultural (Grimes 2014: 259). In the case of pilgrimage, one could well say that the place (landscape, path, etc) 'drives' the ritual complex, that is, it is the focal point, physical and psychosociologically, of the combined ritual actions (Grimes 2014: 242). Thus, 'a ritual is contained by a cosmos and located in one or more geography and ambient ecology ... a system surrounded by and suffused with its ambient societies and constituent cultures' (Grimes 2014: 55).

If, according to DeLattre, ritual is the very 'office of negotiation itself', then it seems that pilgrimage can in many cases be the site of complex negotiations involving commitments and priorities that are cultural, environmental, economic, personal, physical, emotional, and historical (DeLattre 1978: 287). Pilgrims negotiate 'competing claims and attractions of various kinds'—and thus engage in hermeneutical activity—involving geographies, lives, travel schedules, narratives of life and health (DeLattre 1978: 287).

In this way, pilgrimage approaches a kind of political action as it actively interprets reality, celebrating and affirming, as well as reinterpreting and shifting things (DeLattre 1978: 288). Ritual agents interpret self and other in the relationships in which they stand. Based on the assumption that any set of rituals does not resolve problems so much as help affect and renegotiate relations, pilgrimage represents a sliding scale from practice to metaphorical concept. Notions of pilgrimage are consumed, defined and shaped by a network of relations, and may be involved in reshaping practices both personal and communal. In situations of cultural pluralism, this form of negotiation engages multiple cultural and religious narratives, representing a 'ritual geography' (DeLattre 1978: 292). As pilgrims walk territories and float through landscapes, personal and communal narratives are remembered. Place and sound can activate memory and narrative for people, though this will occur differently in oral cultures, where this place-based memory of narrative is key for survival, and for safely finding one's way through the landscape.

Pilgrimages involve particular kinesthetic and tactile senses, and most forms, especially those by foot, bike, horse, by small water craft or boat, are strongly marked by emphatic embodiment (Grimes 2014: 248). Depending on the pilgrim, their intentions, actions, and agents involved, pilgrimages can be empowering or disempowering, affirming or transforming of the status quo, making, unmaking, and remaking meaning (Grimes 2014: 302–317). Some will experience the limits of their own embodiment, and the limitations of their bodies—as feet, knees, backs, etc. give out—as betrayal. Others may take it as a reminder to pay greater attention to a body and soul that has had to take a back seat in a rushed and stressful work life.

In attempting to name 'other-than-human' agents, we may look at space, time, and natural history represented in geology, weather, water, air, earth, plant life, and nonhuman animals. Geological history, seasons, climate and (human) movement shape and recreate landscapes. Paths weave through oceans, along coastline, over mountains, through bogs. Travelers and pilgrims stop to visit markets, churches, farms, and towns, working and marking paths and roads, marked by signs and the occasional monument. The various routes themselves, by land and sea, generate versions of traffic resulting in elemental and biological encounters. Humans travel through landscapes by a variety of means of transport: trains, planes, automobiles, naval vessels, bicycles, buses, and, last but not least, feet. 'Other-than-human' and human actors interact through movement, bodies walking and traveling on paths: soil, land, landscape, plants, water, weather, wind and rain work on bodies as they move and bodies travel and shape the route, rendering notions and narratives of the sacred encountered on the way. It is in these places, land-scapes, movements, and encounters pilgrims may seek, find, and narrate the sacred or the ways in which they increase joy and confront suffering.

Many Roads Lead To Nidaros: A Shifting Network of Routes

Norway's primary territorial access routes were and are coastal, via sea and fjord. Islands off the coast have long had a key place in this geogra-phy as places poised between sea and land (Macfarlane 2012). Selja and Utstein kloster, which lie along the coastal centres route, were transport hubs built in a strategic location between local settlements further into the fjords where ships would pass by on their way up and down the coast. From 1068 to 1170, the seat of the bishop of Bjørgvin was located on the island Selja off the coast. Prior to the arrival of steam and petroleum-driven engines, such locations were centres of traffic and mercantile business. After petroleum-based land and sea routes became dominant, these places became literal backwaters. The *kystleia* (coastal route) was the main route of access to coast and inland, and the region's window to the world (Olsen 2013: 15, 19). The Atlantic was the main travel route for Vikings, traders, and pilgrims, and it is by ship that the first Christian monks and missionaries reached the Norwegian coast. In 2011, the coastal pilgrimage route was reopened by the bishops of the coastal bishoprics during a summer sailing pilgrimage with around one hundred sixty pilgrims aboard (Olsen 2013: 6).

The coastal sea route was easier and more accessible when the weather was cooperative and involved communal travel arrangements. Today, the land route is the primary route for most pilgrims, some going in groups, some alone. While the south to north (Oslo to Trondheim) direction of the land route has become the most commonly traveled, there are other contend-ers. There are routes from Sweden and from the north, and western coastal church groups are considering mapping an overland route from the coast of Møre to Trondheim. Increasingly, the maps of St. Olav Ways from different directions end not far north of Trondheim, giving the impression all that happens in terms of pilgrimage is in the southern part of Norway. 'Pilegrim i Nord',[9] an initiative begun in 2016 and led by a group of Northern Norwegian

9. See Solveig Elisabeth Seines, "Hvor Himmel and Hav Møtes: En Kystpilegrimsseilas-i Olavstradisjonens Kjolvannstripe Langs Kysten i Nord!" (Bodø, 2017), the Facebook group https://nb-no.facebook.com/pilegriminord/, and the Church of Norway's website. https://kirken.no/nn-NO/bispedommer/sor-hologaland/arbeidsomrader1/pilegrim/hva-er-pilegrim-i-nord/.

clergy and church leaders, de-centred and expands the emphasis on some particular land routes in the South of Norway network by highlighting and developing routes to Trondheim from the North of Norway. The initiators, clergy and lay leaders, rented historic fishing cutters and sailboats to remap the old routes.

Many pilgrimages to the relics of saints associate healing with coming into the presence of the remains of the saint. Historically, healing miracles were associated with being near the relics of St. Olav, and were a primary reason to visit. Those who were unable to travel to these sites, however, made do with visiting local churches dedicated to the saint. In Spring 2016 the Oslo pilgrim centre held a one-day conference on the topic of health and pilgrimage. Health is an emerging topic in Norwegian pilgrimage, one that means very different things for different people. One group of scholars attempted to map the 'therapeutic value of pilgrimage' through a 'constructivist grounded theory study' (Warfield, Stanley, and Foxx 2014: 860), and found that pilgrimage can give people who feel that their personal spiritual and physical needs as they are ailing and aging are not given space in the liturgies of the church elsewhere 'narrative framework for coping with their past pain, and after the pilgrimage, [they] reported that they experienced emotional healing regarding their previously silenced pain' (Warfield, Stanley, and Foxx 2014: 861). This matches Anna Fedele's description of Marian pilgrims using narrative as an active ingredient in the healing process (Fedele 2013). Pilgrims on the St. Olav Ways often are newly divorced or separated, somewhat older, and are looking to address some of their burdens through this form of physical/spiritual activity.

Is then the entire pilgrimage network reducible to a private growth and experience provider for pilgrims? My research suggest that pilgrimage has multiple effects on a number of participants in the network beyond the pilgrims themselves: landscape and routes are affected, and so are hosts, clergy, guides, volunteers, musicians, artists, lecturers, technicians, and various other providers of infrastructure. There are many ways to participate, contribute, and gain from the pilgrimage network; from posting on social media to lecturing to local groups, from making documentaries to writing about the experience. Through forging and deepening regional, national and international relations, pilgrimage can strengthen the networks that ground and secure local communities as well as friendly relations with those further afield, thus strengthening, through ritual activity the fabric of democracy and trans-regional relations.

It is tempting to frame the pilgrimage network with a narrow anthropocentric lens. For many pilgrims, especially for those traveling in groups, the relationships between humans seem dominant, and the internal narrative and reflections on them seem in danger of squeezing out anything but the projection of the pilgrim's self upon landscape, history and traveling companions. Studies of pilgrimage generally focus primarily on history, narrative, and the human element of pilgrimage. This is also the case with this pilgrimage, whose reemerging network of routes is centred on the presumed final resting place of St. Olav's remains below an octagonal screen inside Nidaros Cathedral.

Thus it seems easier to focus on ritual as the negotiation of human narratives about history, geography and human and divine actors, such as how migrants, travelers, residents and pilgrims move across territory and space in time, and renegotiate identity and narrative. Are landscape, sanctuary, climate, weather, merely 'ritual places' (Grimes 2014: 256–262), or are they more? Perhaps they are not conscious agents, but they certainly are more than merely backdrop. If seen as part of a network of creaturely relations, the boundaries of being are not neatly distinct. The Norwegian landscape may seem rugged and undomesticated from a tourist's viewpoint, but this romanticized epistemology is somewhat deceptive. Norwegians use the term *kulturlandskap* to refer to arable land, a landscape deeply shaped by cultural forces, agriculture, forestry, climate fluctuations and other factors. That same landscape was previously also shaped by geological forces, glacial ice, its retreat and much later agriculture and aquaculture, fisheries and mining.[10]

Geopsyche, Environmental Engineering and Degradation

> Mixed-up times are overflowing with both pain and joy—with vastly unjust patterns of pain and joy, with unnecessary killing of ongoingness but also with necessary resurgence. (Haraway 2016: 1)

How does one write on pilgrimage in the Anthropocene, oneself an anthropos, about the more and other than human, without being constantly self-referential? Ecological theologians have considered the problem of anthropocentrism over the last few decades. Anthropologists and ethnographers, too, have begun to reflect on the question whether and how the non-human can be heard. Though humans might never be more than 'becoming ventriloquists' (Kirksey, Shapiro, and Brodine 2012) when doing that—a suggestion that feels familiar to many theologians, who are constantly in

10. https://snl.no/kulturlandskap. See also Hessen 2016 and Müller 2016.

danger of becoming ventriloquists of the divine. For even as we write books entitled *How Forests Think*, we are still writing as humans and reporting on human perceptions of the 'beyond the human' (Kohn 2013). What forests think is 'humans imagining what forests think'. Nonetheless, it is worth considering the process of imagining that seeing and representation are 'not exclusively human affairs' (Kohn 2013: 1), that 'life thinks', and that we exist in relation with an entire 'ecology of selves' that include trees, animal predators and dangerous shapeshifters (Kohn 2013: 16). Kohn argues that 'semiosis is intrinsic to life', and thus that 'thoughts are alive', and the world perhaps enchanted (Kohn 2013: 50, 72). Communication in this context is 'not always languagelike' (Kohn 2013: 84).

If human nature is an interspecies relationship that involves relationships to landscapes of various kinds, post-destruction by industrial forestry, melting glaciers, and the like, what could be observed about the various inhabitants of the relational ecology of the cultured landscape (*kulturlandskap*) involved in Norwegian pilgrimage? It is 'soul blindness' that closes human eyes to the 'relational ecology of selves that constitutes the cosmos' (Kohn 2013: 17)? This soul blindness may affect in particular those urban dwellers that go on pilgrimage in larger numbers. The dense relationality of work life, of human bodies and relations folded and compacted leaves little space for inter-species relations. When inter-human relations take up the lion's share of human bandwidth, we may not hear Kohn's panther sneaking through the undergrowth. In the case of pilgrimage, landscapes and places are in communication with the bodies of the pilgrims, and such semiosis occurs through interactions with other beings, in multispecies encounters of 'trans-species pidgin' (Kohn 2013: 144). Still, other pilgrim bodies—the encounters between humans—often crowd out the inter-species encounters.

Is pilgrimage a ritual that allows pilgrims to escape temporarily from what Kohn calls a 'state of monadic isolation [of] soul blindness' to a 'becoming an-other-with-an-other' in a 'range of ways of inhabiting an ecology of selves' (Kohn 2013:140), or is it more focused on *communitas* primarily among pilgrims? In what ways may pilgrims encounter the more than human elements of pilgrimage?

Haraway describes elsewhere the 'becoming-with' that companion species—'ordinary beings-in-encounter'—engage in, in symbioses of many kinds: 'The partners do not precede the knotting; species of all kinds are consequent upon worldly subject- and object-shaping entanglements' (Haraway 2016: 13).

Such 'sympoiesis' indicates 'complex, dynamic, responsive, situated, historical systems', that interact in often unnoticed and unnarrated ways

(Haraway 2016: 58). Here, attempting to conceive of pilgrimage as the possibility for such sympoiesis, I will provide a 'reading that amplifies accounts of the creative, improvisational, and fleeting practices through which plants and insects involve themselves in one another's lives' (Haraway 2016: 69).

Thus, the becoming with and the sympoiesis already occurs, whether it is conscious, narrated, or repressed. Does Kohn's 'soul blindness' reflect a certain inability of selves to perceive 'the soul-stuff of the other souled selves that inhabit the cosmos', of languages beyond the human, leaving the person affected by limited senses unable to consciously reflect on the other than human (Kohn 2013: 117)? And are the ways in which pilgrim bodies force a greater awareness of these relations through the intensity of the interspecies relations—with plants, trees, animals, fish, and geological formations—of walking a path or experiencing wind and waves on the ocean.

Pilgrimage in Norway occurs in landscape that is narrated as part of a national identity—and commercially marketed—as pure, untouched, and majestic, seemingly 'natural'. But interspecies relationships, especially involving humans, have profoundly transformed and are transforming these lands and waters. Climate change manifests as a particularly dramatic phase in interspecies relationships, changing experiences and narratives. If climate change manifests as ecological and social change, then the changing interactions between species are an important part of the ritual expressions of pilgrimage. Writing about it means perceiving and narrating 'possibilities of coexistence within environmental disturbance' (Tsing 2015: 4). Haraway's and Tsing's studies of disturbed landscapes and the relationships that exist within them offers critical examples of how this might be done.

These 'shifting assemblages' of relations in place are also being transformed by the shifts of climate change. Climate change will impact the future shape of this pilgrimage. The Norwegian landscape is a landscape long interacted with, with more to come:

> Disturbance is a change in environmental conditions that causes a pronounced change in an ecosystem. Floods and fires are forms of disturbance, humans and other living things can also cause disturbance. Disturbance can renew ecologies as well as destroy them. (Tsing 2015:160)

The forests of Norway, as elsewhere, may be perceived to be stable, but are in fact rather cyclical, open-ended, and historically dynamic (Tsing 2015: 170). Dag Hessen has traced some of these transformations, specifically the changes in forest and tree coverage, changing fish and wildlife population and retreating glaciers and ice/snow areas (Hessen 2016). Mining products hidden in the sea has facilitated the production of roads, and travel on land and sea. Ice, water and stone shape the landscape, soils and weather, mosses, lichen and grass. Domestic animals, bogs, berries, mushrooms, grow in forests where the paths go.

Water Ways:
Elemental Multispecies Encounters and Trans-species Pidgin

> We think of paths as existing only on land, but the sea has its paths too, though water refuses to take hold marks.... Sea roads are dissolving paths whose passage leaves no trace beyond a wake, a brief turbulence astern.... Sea roads are determined by the shape of the coastline (they bend out to avoid headlands, they dip towards significant ports, archipelagos and skerry guards) as well as by marine phenomena. Surface currents, tidal streams and prevailing winds all offer limits and opportunities for sea travel between certain places. (Macfarlane 2012: 88–89)

Pilgrims traveled both by water and land. Water routes are not permanently visible, they open up and close under the keel of ships. Water is a more capricious element to travel on, but when wind and weather cooperate, it is faster and more flexible, especially in locations dominated by long coastlines. Travelers across sea and land thus shaped pilgrimage then and now, and what they encountered were religious, economic, and cultural goods, practices, techniques, and customs which they adopted, modified and brought home with them. Meanwhile most contemporary travelers, aloft through affordable oil and in fly-over mode, no longer frequent these slower water and land routes, trying to get where they are going as fast as possible.

Today, the St. Olav Ways land routes are more accessible for most travelers, especially for those who want to go alone or in small groups. Yet from 2011 and onwards, two coastal bishops (of Stavanger and Sør-Halogaland) in the Church of Norway presided over a public reopening of the historic sea routes from the south. A few years later, initiatives are being taken to trace a sea route southward from the North, stopping at various now remote seeming island churches.[11] Harald Olsen, a Norwegian historian of pilgrimage, contributes to the sacred geography by describing and remapping the historic oceanic pilgrimages in the North Atlantic and publishing them in

---

11. In 2016 a small number of pilgrims aboard the restored fishing boat *Faxsen* took the route from Bodø to Trondheim during Olsok, and in 2017 another group toured sacred sites in coastal Northern Norway and Lofoten.

book form (Olsen 2013). In 2015, sea kayaker Lars Verket attempted to paddle from Tønsberg to Trondheim, but had to give up and hitch a ride with the steamboat pilgrims at Selja, the site of the first Christian monastery, associated with St. Sunniva. Verket has chronicled this trip—likely the first time the pilgrimage route was traveled by sea kayak—in a book that adds to the literature on the St Olav Ways (Verket 2014).

While pilgrim feet do not get weary on the boats that travel those pilgrim routes, the danger of shipwreck due to inclement weather, and historically at least, piracy, was a real risk on those waterborne routes. Navigation problems, weather, cliffs and other marine troubles made those journeys either quick and easy, or disturbed and potentially lethal.

The rhythms of water are heard, seen and felt. The large ocean swells our *Pilegrim i Nord* group was riding on the Atlantic outer coast of Lofoten and Vesterålen were impossible to ignore in our rather small hundred-year-old wooden fishing boat with a moody motor nearly as old. While pilgrims in more gentle waters and on paths in good weather quickly focus more on their personal, interpersonal and spiritual considerations, the three-to-four-meter waves translated roughly to 4–5 on the Beaufort wind scale and demanded all of our attention.

On other days, the sound of the water as it was split by the keel was gentle, gurgling along the bow of the fishing boat. Water reacts visibly and noticeably to the movements of air and to the heat and light of the sun; it responds quickly and dynamically. Winds change and are affected by land masses. Fjords act like wind channels. When we passed a fjord or a gap between coastal mountains, the wind and water would pick up, and as soon as we came into the shadow of an island off the coast, waves and wind noticeably dropped off, making more possible the task of navigation in large swells. The winds would have both hindered and aided sailors before the advent of the steam boat and the petroleum-based engine. Extensive light during summer allows for long nights on the ocean, while dark and stormy winters are dangerous in cold, dark waters. Headlands might be scenic when we walk on them on land, but they are places when things start moving more quickly and dynamically on the water. Waters and winds that interact around a headland can be dramatic even without the added effect of inclement weather.

There are waves whose movement feels like an invitation to a waltz, at times with increasing or decreasing energy and frequency, and others, when you begin to worry your dance partner is going a little nuts. One day the skipper asked us to take seasickness tablets and stay below deck since the deck was so exposed that it was irresponsible for passengers to be on deck. Within the old, tight spaces, several of us envisioned the difficulty of getting on deck in time in the case of a shipwreck. We contemplated the possibility that this might be a last journey. And in that sense, it may have been a pilgrim moment, recognizing the dangers of the journey and of life. Had anybody fallen in the cold waters without a drysuit, their likelihood of surviving would have been slim, even with a coast guard station nearby. The boat would have been unable to turn around or even stop and navigate safely in heavy seas. Even so, or perhaps because of that, it was one of the highlights of our trip. Several of the pilgrims considered it their most memorable experience at reflection time before the group said goodbye and disbanded into various different directions. Reminders of the realities of the coastal culture we saw in every port we stopped, of fishermen rowing their boats in high waves, of ship wrecks, and markers for drowned sailors on the coast and in churches were made all too real.

The hermeneutics of wind, wave, ocean and coast as influenced by the travels of sun and moon is a highly complex set of rhythms interacting with each other. Repetition of this pilgrimage by water would be unrealistic for the average pilgrim, unless they already own a sailboat or larger motor boat and have solid navigation experience. Such a journey requires maps, positioning and navigation systems, as well as the ability of interpreting the correspondence of map and territory in varying conditions.

Norwegian engineering now focuses on drilling platforms and ships and other oil extraction technologies. Today's ocean-going craft are highly specialized movable platforms, tankers, drilling ships, floating fish farm barges, and ferries binding together the ragged ranges, carved by glaciers and weather. The coast is dotted with marine culture, salmon farms, petroculture, and other marine infrastructure. Coastal transportation has in some places been replaced by expensive under-fjord tunnels, bridges, and other coastal engineering projects that aim to straighten out and cut through the landscape, rather than adjusting to its curves and moods. Thus, petroleum-based transportation continues to change landscape, transport logistics, economies, ecologies, population and settlement patterns in Norway.

And this long, hard-to-navigate land is not a land designed by an engineer looking for efficient travel routes. Generations of fishing folk told their priests they would not appreciate it if 'the sea was no more' as imagined in the Book of Revelations. For a heaven without an ocean was a vision of heaven undesirable to them. Yet, they may not recognize the efforts of their grandchildren, engineers doing their best to level out 'every valley shall be exalted and every mountain laid low', eliminating the constraints oceans put on humans. Efforts to put the elements of the landscapes Norwegians are so proud of into subservience to human designs highlights anthropocentrism and fully pushes other than human parts of the network further into a scenic backdrop to be managed and controlled at will. Contemporary cheap oil commuter patterns render these landscapes mostly an annoyance on the quicker, faster and safer way to work and leisure. It is also this mindset that some pilgrims want to take a break from.

Islands as Connecting Hubs of the Water Ways

Islands have a particular place in this system of land and water routes; they are sites for monasteries that are both inaccessible and accessible, form their own ecologies and economies of relationship with land and sea. Locals and tourists take the time to bob on the waves, ferrying between and around islands. The Lewis chess pieces, which were found on what is now one of the more remote places in the North Sea on the Outer Hebrides, ended up on the Isle of Lewis because the island lay along a trading route between Norway and the British Isles. The mystery of their presence on Lewis reveals old trade routes where goods like ivory show up, suggesting the existence of networks of exchange of far greater complexity than most modern people imagine.

The Irish monks were famous religious travelers and pilgrims, and the Vikings that ruled Lewis for several centuries roamed from Kiev to Jerusalem and the British Isles, Iceland, Greenland, and beyond. The sea is a quick connector, a formidable adversary, and a wet grave to many. St. Olav was one of those travelers, leaving as a pagan, and eventually returning as a Christian intent on introducing Christian laws and using the new faith to unite the many fiefdoms as a unified Christian nation. The Christian faith here, as elsewhere, has community and faith-building effects, often intentionally used by power players such as kings and other rulers to generate cohesion in the presence of divisive tribal and regional forces.

Crucial in Olav Tryggvason's quest to establish Christianity more firmly was a saint who came from the isles across the ocean. St. Sunniva, perhaps an Irish princess, as the name indicates, was thought to have settled on the island of Selja, also the site of a monastery likely built by Irish or British monastics. For it was thence that Christianity first entered the lands now known as Norway, by sea. In the case of Irish monks, fearless ocean sailors who were not just pilgrims but also missionaries and settlers, pilgrimage and migration intersect. Pilgrims generally use routes that are merchant and royal routes, migration routes, often shared paths by travelers of various kinds.

Paths on Land:
Place, Movement and its Impact on the Social Body

There is a starkly physical relationship that shapes the experience of the walking pilgrim. Casual walkers may feel greater connection with the places they amble through, able to think and encounter landscape and people. But longer distances can have a different effect on the body, relegating the conscious reflection process to the background and foregrounding the noises of the body when exhaustion and pain take over (Solnit 2000).

Blisters, foot and leg pains, and the power of gravity on the pilgrim's body are major factors affecting the journey. People walk with pain and through pain. Many long-distance pilgrims report that their hopes of quiet, peaceful reflections about God, their spiritual path, their faith and enjoyment of the landscape and other people can be harshly pushed aside by the forced focus on the body's functions and pains that invade every thought—and demand care.

Pilgrimages often proceed on harsh surfaces that are not made to accommodate human feet and distract from the berries one could pluck, churches one could visit, or diversions that could be worth it. The path and the gravity of bodies exert a harsh regiment that reduces the ability to concentrate on other experiences. If pilgrimages meander a sacred landscape, then that sacred is generally a 'wounded sacred' (Wallace 2005), that is, it is a scarred or polluted landscape, without losing its importance, integrity or the need to protect it. Unlike a hike in the Norwegian mountains, the pilgrim route does not hide its proximity to human infrastructure and settlement; there is no pretense that the pilgrim walks a pristine path.

The guided pilgrimage I participated in during the summer of 2014 was overwhelmed by 'body noise', marking an emphatic embodiment where foot and hip pains significantly shaped my experience of the pilgrims as well as my relationships with them. Indeed, my body pain became an agent itself that galvanized and deepened relations with the others, and stripped away all my defenses. The experience served to further drive home questions about what one sees, discovers, and relates to, depending on how the body engages with the pilgrimage network and especially in movement along the path and at sites. Happiness, for many other long-distance pilgrims, seems to come through their focus being forced into the microcosm that is directly in and around them. It reduces the distracting complexity of their everyday world to the (seeming) simplicity of bodily functions.

Clear and frequent signs along the route are crucial to the thriving of many pilgrims, much more so than for the hiker, who often carries a detailed map, compass, and may have the trip planned in detail. This is more difficult to accomplish for pilgrims who often go through territory where signs are less visible than the ubiquitous red T of the Norwegian Tourist Association (DNT) in the backcountry. Over the last few years, however, this has been a distinction that has become blurred: hikers, tourists, and pilgrims often overlap. The DNT, the Norwegian *Tourist* Association was initially founded to make Norwegian nature more accessible to those who did not live there, which included foreigners. Over the course of its history, however, it has served mostly Norwegians, who are the most vigorous users of its hiking paths. The newest editions of DNT hiking maps include pilgrimage routes in a standout color and with a specific label. In fact the DNT has become a collaborative partner of those developing the pilgrimage routes and describes them in hiking software and books.[12]

Several pilgrims admitted to me that they broke out in tears and cursed, experiencing a kind of situational despair when they could not find the next way marker or sign, or found that they had to backtrack because they had walked the wrong way for a while. This despair vanished quickly as soon as the next marker on the route was found. The importance of a road that is reliable and does not turn into an orienteering task is often described as a key component of a good experience. Unlike hiking trails, pilgrimage routes often go through territories with a larger variety of route options than one finds in remote hiking and skiing territories. On the DNT maps, the hiking route is often the only passable foot path, or the only route traversing a territory, while pilgrimage routes more often involve agricultural routes, gravel roads, and asphalt multiuse paths along main traffic thoroughfares. This greater dependence on the route and the ability to correctly interpret the signs along the route can take up a significant amount of the pilgrim's consciousness.

Pilgrims along the Gudbrandsdalen, the most used and most developed path in the network so far, can increasingly enjoy signs on matters of geology, natural history, cultural and religious history, folklore and even art exhibits installed on the route. That is, the inner monologue or the conversations between pilgrims are increasingly supplemented by additional input that helps explain the landscape and history one walks through, a kind of modern replacement of the oral history and folklore it reports on (etymologies of notable landscape features, etc.) Even those pilgrims who are uninterested in

12. As an example may serve the following article showing an organized tour under the umbrella of the DNT Gudbrandsdalen region but clearly marked as a pilgrimage: https://gudbrandsdalen.dnt.no/aktiviteter/88133/844566/.

the figure of St. Olav or even Nidaros Cathedral often experience a kind of 'crescendo' (in the words of one pilgrim) of messages or experiences related to the goal as they draw closer to the end of the road.

My own spiritual experiences in wayless wilderness and on the paths of U.S. national parks, included encounters with wildlife—caribou, grizzlies, eagles—and the visceral impression landscapes I traveled through made on me. The small miracles many pilgrims report seem to be 'Emmaus moments'—encountering Christ unrecognized—that have to do with surprising synchronicities of human kindness, of being given a bottle of water, of finding help of the one or other kind along the roadside, receiving a kind word or some physical or spiritual wisdom that makes the journey just a little bit easier. Pilgrims steeped in the Christian tradition may report that this is the way they imagine the original fellowship of the apostles where all things were held in common.

Climate Change and Pilgrimage: Walking for Interspecies Democracy

When do pilgrims strengthen an economy, and when do they threaten to destroy it, and the ecosystems it is based on? Landscape and travel across it are affected by the traffic that pilgrims bring and infrastructure that accommodates their travel. It is of course not only in tourism and pilgrimage that this form of self-narration and reconceptualization occurs. It happens just as easily when those bodies engage their own societies. Kari Norgaard has explored the dynamics of Norwegian narrations of self under the conditions of climate change in a petroleum-driven economy. Despite the realization that climate change is beginning to change their life world, people in Norgaard's research setting state that they 'live in one way and think in another. We learn to think in parallel. It's a skill, an art of living' (Marshall 2014: 83). Furthermore, as George Marshall summarizes,

> Norwegians have particularly good reasons for ignoring climate change. Norway's cultural identity, Norgaard explained, is based around a mythic narrative that it is a small and humble nation that lives simply and close to nature. Norwegians pride themselves on being honest and conscientious global citizens and their government speaks often of being a world leader on climate change. (Marshall 2014: 83)

Despite Norway's leadership role when it comes to climate, it is a very ambivalent one. Like residents of Alaska, each Norwegian citizen and resident benefits from the oil economy, thanks to the massive state owned and administered *Oljefondet* oil fund,

> which now includes a two-billion dollar stake in Alberta's tar sands. All in all, Norway is a spectacularly large contributor to climate change and, thanks to its egalitarian traditions, it has shared that responsibility across its entire population. (Marshall 2014: 83)

Norgaard found that Norwegians had a high stake in a selective myth that itself is 'a political act'. That is, 'people chose not to know too much in order to maintain their cultural identity as responsible citizens' (Marshall 2014: 84). This discrepancy, certainly not unique to Norwegians, is merely an example that pertains to this study and offers another set of considerations as pilgrimage is reimagined in Norway.

The *Green Pilgrimage Network* was founded to counteract the ecological bomb that large numbers of pilgrims represent when the sustainability of a place and region is not considered.[13] It is often ignored that pilgrimage, just like other forms of tourism, produces trash and represents heightened use of resources. Compared to the often invisible pollution of the cruise ships that wind their ways through Norwegian fjords in increasing numbers and that process and dump human waste offshore when they head out in deeper waters, the ecological footprint may be relatively small, or invisible, but it does exist. Even growing numbers of pilgrims traveling by foot affect the landscapes they travel through. What sustainable pilgrimage might look like in Norway is still emerging.

One of the ways in which pilgrimage has been connected to climate change has been around water. At times, pilgrims will carry small quantities of water from their home watersheds to conferences, something that has become somewhat of a tradition in some ecumenical meetings. At a conference in Sweden on *The Future of Life in the Arctic* in the fall of 2015, one of the delegates commented on the fact that, sadly the mixture of water drops brought to Storforsen by the attendants would be undrinkable, as various of these streams were heavily polluted. That water ritual of sharing and gathering the waters indeed shows the reality of what is happening to our waters. Water is significant in many religious rituals, it is prominent in biblical narrative and central to the Christian sacraments, especially baptism. This gathering of drops from various bodies represents an interspecies democracy where the water symbolises an interspecies participant in the UN

---

13 See http://www.greenpilgrimage.org/en/.

Paris climate meeting. The sacramental force of water remains, but pollution of water, which signifies a lack of respect towards its inherent sacredness, affects the sacrament. Perhaps this experience also highlights the significance of the concept of a sacred well, such as historically has attracted those who seek healing and pilgrims.

Klimapilegrim 2015 was a series of Norwegian climate action events that aimed to think climate change and pilgrimage together and raise awareness of their interconnection. It was arranged during the summer of 2015 and intended to raise awareness of the issues of climate change leading up to the UN COP meeting in Paris. Two officers of the Church of Norway, Knut Hallen and Per Ivar Våje, came up with the initial idea over a cup of coffee, and then proceeded to involve a variety of NGOs in a pilgrimage that involved large swaths across Norway.[14] The actions involved in this set of activities involved 200 events, 7,000 participants who together walked around 60,000 kilometers and gathered around 9,000 signatures (Våje 2015).

During these events, many local pilgrims from all of Norway became involved in *Klimapilegrim 2015*. Lay and clergy pilgrims gathered drops of water from various bodies of water throughout the country into several bottles that were then transported via a relay on foot, bike and train to the 2015 UN Climate Summit in Paris. Two bottles of water, one gathered at Selje, the site of the historic first bishop's seat and the well of St. Sunniva, and another from the far North of the North Cape, were brought together under the motto *Jeg vil ha en rettferdig klimapolitikk der Norge bidrar med mindre utslipp og mer penger* (I want just climate policies where Norway contributes with fewer emissions and more money) to represent the 'species' of water among the human bodies gathering. While it was a symbolic ritual act, it attempted to raise awareness in Norwegian society regarding climate change.

Further actions involved a high point with possibly the first truly interreligious pilgrimage arrangement in Norway when pilgrims brought the bottles of water into Oslo. There, part of the way involved representatives of the Church of Norway, local Muslim, and Sikh communities for a short common pilgrimage from Grønland, a centre of immigrant culture in Oslo, to the Norwegian Parliament. Speeches and performances marked a joint purpose among the religious communities. Water from the streams of Norway carried via land all the way to Paris to bring the message of troubled waters and lands, urging the world for action on climate change.

---

14 Knut Hallen, personal communication.

The social effectiveness of rituals is notoriously difficult to assess. Do these pilgrimages galvanize sustained action rather than facilitate improvised short-term gestures and public relations opportunities? The pilgrimage network presents the various participants in its rituals with at least the possibility of having both religious and political significance. This essay attempted to map a field of relations in which the more than human relationality and affective ecological relations can be mapped and described using an affective epistemology. The rituals involved in the pilgrimage network consist of 'crossing and dwelling' and allowing instances of affective communitas through heightening opportunities for narrating interspecies relations and heightened awareness on the historic transformations of climate, landscape and peoples. These possibilities for perceiving affective communitas can heighten awareness as well as challenge the means and modes of a petroleum economy and transport, ethnocentric definitions of democratic citizenship and national identity, and species and landscapes other than the human.

References

Bowman, Marion, and Tina Sepp (2019), 'Caminoisation and Cathedrals: Replication, the Heritagisation of Religion, and the Spiritualisation of Heritage'. *Religion*, 49/1: 74–98. https://doi.org.10.1080/0048721X.2018.1515325.

Castles, Stephen, Hein de Haas, and Mark J. Miller (2014), *The Age of Migration: International Population Movements in the Modern World*. 5th ed., New York: Guilford Press. https://doi.org/10.24201/edu.v17i1.1136.

DeLattre, Roland (1978), 'Ritual Resourcefulness and Cultural Pluralism', *Soundings: An Interdisciplinary Journal*, 61/3: 281–301.

Fedele, Anna (2013), *Looking for Mary Magdalene: Alternative Pilgrimage and Ritual Creativity at Catholic Shrines in France*, Oxford: Oxford University Press. https://doi.org/10.1093/acprof:oso/9780199898404.001.0001.

Flatø, Emil (2017), 'Norge Tar Av: En reise til hjertet av den norske flyavhengigheten'. *Morgenbladet*, 28 April.

Grimes, Ronald L. (2014), *The Craft of Ritual Studies*. Oxford: Oxford University Press. https://doi.org/10.1093/acprof:oso/9780195301427.001.0001.

Haraway, Donna J. (2016), *Staying with the Trouble: Making Kin the Chthulucene*. Durham: Duke University Press. https://doi.org/10.1215/9780822373780.

Hessen, Dag O. (2016), *Landskap i Endring*. Oslo: Pax.

Kirksey, Eben, Nicholas Shapiro, and Maria Brodine (2012), 'Introduction.' *Environmental Humanities* 1, 1–24 *The Multispecies Salon*, vol. 1, ed, Eben Kirksey. Durham, NC: Duke University Press. https://doi.org/10.1111/amet.12029_16.

Kohn, Eduardo (2013), *How Forests Think: Toward and Anthropology Beyond the Human*. Berkeley: University of California Press. https://doi.org/10.1525/california/9780520276109.001.0001.

Legat, Alice (2008), 'Walking Stories; Leaving Footprints'. in *Ways of Walking: Ethnography and Practice on Foot*, eds. Tim Ingold and Jo Lee Vergunst. Anthropological Studies of Creativity and Perception, 35–49. Aldershot: Ashgate. https://doi.org/10.1111/j.1469-8676.2010.00117_9.x.

Lochtefeld, James G. (2010), *God's Gateway: Identity and Meaning in a Hindu Pilgrimage Place*. Oxford: Oxford University Press, 2010.

Macfarlane, Robert (2012), *The Old Ways: A Journey on Foot*. London: Penguin,

Marshall, George (2014), *Don't Even Think About It: Why Our Brains Are Wired to Ignore Climate Change*. London: Bloomsbury. https://doi.org/10.1080/10477845.2018.1470432.

Moore, Stephen D. and Mayra Rivera, eds. (2011), *Planetary Loves: Spivak, Postcoloniality, and Theology*. New York: Fordham University Press. https://doi.org/10.1111/j.1467-9418.2012.01071.x.

Müller, Reidar (2016), *Det Som Ble Norge: Om Fjell, Is Og Liv Gjennom 2902 Millioner År*. Oslo: Aschehoug.

Olsen, Harald (2013), *Havets Pilegrimer*. Oslo: Verbum.

Oviedo, Lluis, Scarlett de Courcier, and Miguel Farias (2014), 'Rise of Pilgrims on the Camino to Santiago: Sign of Change or Religious Revival?' *Review of Religious Research*, 56/3: 433–442. https://doi.org/10.1007/s13644-013-0131-4.

Picard, David, and Michael Di Giovine (2014), 'Introduction: Through Other Worlds'. in *Tourism and the Power of Otherness: Seductions of Difference*, eds. David Picard and Michael Di Giovine. Tourism and Cultural Change, 1–28. Bristol: Channel View Publications. https://doi.org/10.21832/9781845414177-003.

Seines, Solveig Elisabeth (2017), 'Hvor Himmel and Hav Møtes: En Kystpilegrimsseilas-i Olavstradisjonens Kjolvannstripe Langs Kysten i Nord!' Bodø.

Solnit, Rebecca. *Wanderlust: A History of Walking*. New York: Penguin, 2000.

Söderlund, Staffan, and Marie Sjöstöm (2016), *St. Olavsleden: Pilgrimsfärd Från Hav Till Hav—En Guide*. Växsjö: Vidmarksbiblioteket.

Taylor, Charles (2007), *A Secular Age*. Cambridge, MA: Belknap Press.

Tsing, Anna Lowenhaupt (2012), 'Blasted Landscapes (and the Gentle Arts of Mushroom Picking)'. *Environmental Humanities* 1: 87–109 *The Multispecies Salon*, vol. 1, ed. Eben Kirksey. Durham, NC: Duke University Press. https://doi.org/10.1215/9780822376989-005.

Tsing, Anna Lowenhaupt (2012), 'Unruly Edges: Mushrooms as Companion Species', *Environmental Humanities* 1: 141–54. https://doi.org/10.1215/22011919-3610012.

Tsing, Anna Lowenhaupt (2015), *The Mushroom at the End of the World: On the Possibility of Life in Capitalist Ruins*. Princeton: Princeton University Press.

Turner, Victor, and Edith Turner (1978), *Image and Pilgrimage in Christian Culture: Anthropological Perspectives*. New York: Columbia University Press.

Tweed, Thomas (2006), *Crossing and Dwelling : A Theory of Religion*. Cambridge, MA: Harvard University Press. https://doi.org/10.4159/9780674044517.

Vaje, Per Ivar (2015), 'Klimapilegrim 2015: Pa Vei Til Klimarettferighet'. Skaperverk og Bærekraft. Oslo.

Verket, Lars (2014), *Padlepilegrim: Fra Tønsberg Til Nidaros*. Stavanger: Kai Hansen Trykkeri.

Wallace, Mark I. (2005), *Finding God in the Singing River: Christianity, Spirit, Nature*. Minneapolis: Fortress.

Warfield, Heather, Baker, Stanley, and Foxx, Sejal Parikh (2014), 'The Therapeutic Value of Pilgrimage: A Grounded Theory Study.' *Mental Health, Religion & Culture*, 17/8: 860–875. https://doi.org/10.1080/13674676.2014.936845.

Webb, Diana (2002), *Medieval European Pilgrimage*. London: Palgrave.

Winroth, Anders (2011), *The Conversion of Scandinavia: Vikings, Merchants, and Missionaries in the Making of Northern Europe*. New Haven: Yale University Press. https://doi.org/10.1111/j.1468-2265.2012.00790_75.x.

About the Author

Marion Grau is professor of systematic theology, ecumenism and missiology at MF Norwegian School of Theology, Religion, and Society in Oslo, Norway. Her teaching interests are in constructive theology and her current research projects include the redevelopment of pilgrimage and the reshaping of identity in Norway and a Theology of petroleum economies and climate change in the Northern Hemisphere. She is the author of *Rethinking Theological Hermeneutics: Hermes, Trickster, Fool* (Palgrave MacMillan, 2014), *Rethinking Mission in the Postcolony: Salvation, Society, and Subversion* (T&T Clark/Continuum, 2011), *Of Divine Economy: Refinancing Redemption* (T&T Clark/Continuum, 2004).

5. How to Do Things with Rituals, or Disrupting Protestant Lutheran Theology: Converting Refugees and the Eucharist

Gitte Buch-Hansen

Introduction

The Significance of Eucharist Elements: The Host and the Hosts

'Something elementary and true characterizes the way that A (young, male, Afghan asylum seeker) hosts the Eucharist. The word that accompanies the bread is simply: "Jesus!" Well, that is what it is. I like it. No need to wrap it up in a lot of liturgical terms. I always attempt to get into the line which he serves.'
Fragment of conversation during church coffee, picked up from a young Danish female member of the congregation.

Eucharist Choreograph: Sunday Service in the Apostles' Church

If you happen to spend a Sunday morning in the socially and ethnically diverse west end of central Copenhagen, we suggest that you drop in for a service in the Apostles' Church.[1] Gentrification characterizes the area: smart cafés and fancy restaurants gradually replace the pizzerias and the shops

---

1. 'We' are the author plus Marlene Ringgaard Lorensen, Professor in Practical Theology, Faculty of Theology, University of Copenhagen. Our research project, *Consumed Identities: Ritualized Food and the Negotiation of National Identity in the Evangelical Lutheran Church in Denmark* formed part of the project *Reassembling Democracy: Ritual as Cultural Resource* and was financed by the Norwegian Research Council. Our methodological considerations as well as some of the 'data'—that is, the migrants' life-stories—have previously been presented in Buch-Hansen, Lorensen, and Felter 2015 and Buch-Hansen 2018. However, the perspective on and the analysis of the 'data' in the present essay differs from our previous work.

with vegetables, couscous, and olives that served the immigrant workers from Turkey, Pakistan, and Morocco who took over the small apartments the working class left behind, when during the 1960s the latter settled in single-family estates in the suburbs. The church may be difficult to find, as only the bell tower guides you into the backyard where the congregation gathers.

If you are on time, the room will be half-empty. Most of the people that are present are family groups: either Danish middle-aged couples decently dressed up for the service sitting up front, or families of Middle-Eastern origin occupying the pews in the midsection of the church, which are equipped for simultaneous interpreting. However, within the first ten minutes of the service, the rest of the church will soon be filled with young, Danish hipsters (probably students or artists), families with small children settling with blankets and toys in the left corner near the entrance, and some single, elderly, Danish people from the neighbourhood finding a free seat. Half way through the service, a group of male youths of Middle-Eastern origin will tiptoe in and take their seats at the back. If you ask a local person whether these guys are unaware of the starting point of the service, he or she will explain to you that, with public transportation, it is impossible for the asylum seekers to reach the service in due time because the reception centres are placed in distant, depopulated regions.[2]

When at the end of the service the ritual of the Eucharist draws near, two to three hundred people will be present in the room.[3] With a few exceptions,

2.   We use the term 'asylum seeker' for a person who has applied for the formal status as 'refugee'. According to the UNHCR's Refugee Convention (cf. http://www.unhcr.org/about-us/background/4ec262df9/1951-convention-relating-status-refugees-its-1967-protocol.html) 'real' refugees are granted asylum. For the sake of linguistic variation, we sometimes use the term '(im)migrants' as a shared category for both the applicants and the accepted cases.

3.   The Eucharist, also called the Lord's Table, constitutes, together with Baptism, the two *sacraments*, which all Christian denominations share (Christian theologians often hesitate to use the term 'ritual'). To Christians, the performance of the Eucharist is grounded in the Bible. In the accounts of the *Last Supper*, which Jesus shares with his disciples, he instructs them how to commemorate him. He identifies the bread and the wine, which are consumed at the table, with his body and blood, respectively. His words, which are now part of the Eucharist's liturgy is found in the apostle Paul's First Letter to the Corinthians: 'This is my body that is for you. Do this in remembrance of me' and 'This cup is the new covenant in my blood. Do this, as often as you drink it, in remembrance of me!' (1 Cor 11:24–25). Below we will return to the specific history of the Eucharist in the Lutheran Evangelical Church in Denmark (officially abbreviated to the ELCD).

everyone in the church participates in the ritual; only the elderly, Danish people, for whom the Eucharist is still an extraordinary element in the service, may watch the event from the pews. The traditional arrangement of the room with two sections of pews separated by the centre aisle divides the participants into three long rows: one in the centre, two along the sides. Consequently, the socially and ethnically homogeneous groups at the pews—Danes, Nigerians, Iraqis, Iranians, Afghans, Kurds—are blended when they reach the Lord's Table. However, not everyone who comes to the altar receives the bread and the wine. Some restrict their participation to the blessing from the priest. They may be migrants in the process of converting from Islam to Christianity, or non-Christians who participate for the experience of community. Due to the high number of people participating in the Eucharist, the minister needs assistance with the distribution of bread and wine. Three persons representing the gendered and ethnic diversity of the attendees act as co-hosts. However, it has not always been this way.

In the early summer of 2014, three months after we had begun our fieldwork in the Apostles' Church, we presented our interpretation of the 'data' that we had collected during our participatory observations, to the Danish core of the congregation. Among the more problematic issues to which we drew attention was the relationship between the welcoming Danish host(s) and the migrants as welcomed guests. We explained that although hospitality creates a relationship between host and guest, hospitality without reciprocity generates debts, dependency and hierarchy. We argued that the perfect host has to create possibilities for becoming the guest him or herself. We only presented our observations and reflections, but left it to the congregation to decide whether—and, if so, how—they wanted to act on them. As their response, the church council now takes care that the hosts of the Eucharist represent the diversity in the pews.

The statement placed at the beginning of this paragraph reflects the congregation's assent to the new combination of hosts at the Lord's Table. With the introduction of the novel practice, assisting at the Eucharist has become an important goal to which converts aspire. Those who have recently been baptized eagerly exercise the liturgical phrase, 'This is the body of Christ'. When, in an interview, we asked the young Afghan asylum seeker, to whom the opening epigraph refers, about his experience as a first-time host, he answered that he felt so 'warm inside'.

At the close of this essay, we will return to this Afghan man and suggest an explanation for his emotional reaction. In the meantime, we will, with the aid of ritual theory, try to shed some light on the social effects as well as the theological outcome of the changes in the Eucharist that the presence of migrants at the Lord's Table, provoked. But before we move on, presentation of some prerequisite information is necessary: the particular Danish context of our case and the methodology on which our 'data' is based.

Wafer Host or Homemade Bread? Ritual Theo-Politics

When in early 2014 we visited the Apostles' Church for the first time, the bread distributed in the Eucharist was a Middle Eastern thin, pancake-like bread. A young Danish man, who was volunteering in the church, remembered one particular Sunday, when the thin bread happened to be infused with, as he said, 'not the Holy Spirit alone', but also various spices. Probably, no one had planned it to be that way, as he explained. Most likely, someone from the congregation had just bought the bread in a nearby store on his or her way to the service. Because of the many shops around the church with goods of Middle Eastern origin, the bread just happened to taste of cumin and garlic. In this way, but quite accidentally, the body of Christ was contextualized according to the ethnicity of the parish. This unexpected stimulation of the senses invited new interpretations of the Eucharist. The minor displacement in the ritual reminded the young man of the Church's Middle Eastern origins and its present international character with the effect that, to him, the Lord's Table expanded beyond the particular moment and place.

With Proustian effects like this, it may come as a surprise that at the same time as the Apostles' Church changed its habits with regard to the hosting of the Eucharist, it gave up serving the Middle Eastern bread and returned to the crispy white wafer with the print of the crucified Christ. As no one could explain the change, it did not reflect thorough theological considerations. Probably, someone had forgotten to buy bread for the Eucharist and a packet with oblates was at hand in the sacristy. For the sake of convenience, it just stayed that way. Haphazardly or not, recent developments in the Evangelical Lutheran Church in Denmark (ELCD) rendered the return to the wafer host difficult for us to understand. The modern history of the Eucharist in a Danish context may explain our puzzlement.

During the 1980s, younger generations among church-going Danes began to participate in the Eucharist as an integrated part of their worship. As part of this new practice, families would take even their small children to the altar in order to receive the bread and (a sip of) the wine. Whether this development was motivated by a New Age-inspired quest for spirituality and mystery, or represented a striving for a stronger religious identity provoked by the new presence of Islam in the townscape, nobody knows. Anyway, in response to this change of behaviour, the Eucharist was included in the Ordo—that is, the guidelines for the ordinary service—when the ELCD revised its liturgy in 1992. Before the reform, the performance of the Eucharist was reserved for the High Mass. Now it was a mandatory element in every service. This change troubled theologians and ministers of a more traditional Protestant Lutheran inclination. With the new Ordo, they sensed a displacement of the centre of worship from the sermon and the proclamation of the Gospel toward the ritual: after all, if the promise of forgiveness was believed, the Eucharist with its enactment of the absolution of sins seemed superfluous. In addition, many Christians experienced participation in the Eucharist as a public confession of private sins, which prevented even stable churchgoers from attending the Lord's Table.

The new Ordo has had as its effect that the Eucharist has become a site where Christian theology and identity are now negotiated. Within the ELCD, two opposing tendencies may be seen. On the one hand, we find congregations in which tradition is emphasized and the use of the oblate with the print of the crucified Christ is claimed to be mandatory. On the other hand, we see small-scale ritual experiments within the framework of the Ordo. Bread, often made using local or fairly traded 'green' produce, is used in place of the printed wafer. In addition, these different practices often reflect a gendered choice: female ministers tend to make and serve bread, whereas their male colleagues prefer the traditional host. The materiality of the medium—the homemade, chewy bread or the printed, crispy wafer host—may stimulate different understandings of the ritual. When the bread is used, connotations of a ritualized meal are strengthened. Moreover, when the bread is made of locally produced grain, a chthonic element is added. In this case, the Eucharist tends to summon people around a generous, creator God, who upholds life in its various forms. In contrast with this interpretation, the print of the cross on the wafer host reduces the semantic surplus of the ritual and safeguards the traditional, Christological interpretation of the ritual as the place of confession and absolution of sin. When the participant consumes the wafer with the image of the crucified Christ, his or her identity as a sinner is internalized. The threshold for participation in the ritual also differs: whereas the consumption of the printed host presupposes Christian beliefs, it is possible to interpret the broken bread along several interreligious trajectories.

We interpreted the practice that first met us in the Apostles' Church, when the body of Christ was still offered in the form of Middle Eastern bread, in line with the new, to our mind, more permissive tradition. To us, this particular performance of the Eucharist appeared as an open invitation that united the congregation, including those non-Christians who for various reasons were present during the service. The thin pancake-like bread bought in a nearby shop was precisely as 'local' as that made of home-grown bio-dynamic spelt. But why did the congregation then change its practice and return to the traditional wafer host? Whereas our initial participatory observations left this question unexplained, the in-depth interviews that we later conducted with migrants suggested an answer. However, the explanation was more complex than the sketch of the two tendencies in Danish theology, which we have called the liberal and the conservative, could account for. Although the performance of the Eucharist in the Apostles' Church now looked like the ritual performed by the more conservative traditions within the ELCD, our work demonstrated that the participants—at least, the asylum seekers and refugees—understood it quite differently. The migrants' appropriation of the Eucharist represents a foretaste of the way that globalization is affecting the ELCD.

Consumed Identities:
A Methodological Recipe for Culinary Research

According to the National Constitution, the Danish State supports the ELCD legally (and economically). This corresponds with the fact that the vast majority of the population, 75.9 per cent on the 1st of January 2017, belong to the ELCD.[4] Nevertheless, half a century of various waves of migration has challenged the role of this monolithic institution in the Danish society; the intimate link between national identity, history, ethnicity, and religion has been disturbed. The overriding aim of our research project, *Consumed Identities: Ritualized Food and the Negotiation of National Identity in the Evangelical Lutheran Church in Denmark*, was to shed light on this situation.

In opposition to the majority of congregations in the ELCD, the parishioners in the Apostles' Church include newcomers of radically different cultural backgrounds—among them asylum seekers and refugees from Iraq, Iran, and Afghanistan—in its activities and spiritual life. Consequently, fieldwork in this particular church seemed an obvious choice as a starting point for our research project.

When designing our fieldwork, we had in mind that the sharing of a meal is a very basic act of ritual action, which establishes or breaks down hierarchies and boundaries. Consequently, we chose to focus on the distribution

---

4. http://www.km.dk/folkekirken/kirkestatistik/folkekirkens-medlemstal/.

of food (of all kinds) and the eating patterns in and around the congregation in the Apostles' Church: the provision of food, the preparation of meals, the distribution of invitations, the participation in the meals, as well as the left-overs: the dishwashing, the sweeping of the floor and so forth. In our study, we visited both 'ordinary' meals with a low degree of ritualization and participated in the highly ritualized Eucharist.

Our study, which was carried out during 2014 (and resumed in the spring of 2017), was triangulated through a combination of (i) participant observations and (ii) in-depth interviews with individual newcomers in the congregation. Both of these ways of collecting information were followed by (iii) feedback on our interpretations of the 'data' from the congregation as in the above-mentioned example with the discussion about the co-hosts. With regard to our interviews, we were acutely aware of the importance of perspective and discussed how we could let the migrants' experiences be the starting point for our conversation. In order to distribute power more equally, we provided each of our interviewees with a digital camera and asked them to take a series of photographs, which would represent their life in and around the Apostles' Church. These pictures and the stories that the migrants associated with them, became the starting point for our conversation about their conversion as well as their encounter with this particular church and the ELCD in general.

When we began interviewing the asylum seekers and refugees in the Apostles' Church, we looked forward to positive accounts of the many meals which, in various forms were served and shared in the life of the church. We expected to hear that the meals were an important element in the bonding of the congregation and that the food made the church an attractive place for newcomers. Therefore, it came as a surprise that the meals were also situations in which conflicts of ethnic, social, and gendered origin were articulated. The more so, as our initial observations had not made us aware of these problems; to us, the atmosphere around the meals appeared friendly and welcoming. Was this difference in perception due to the fact that we, after all, were cultural outsiders to the community of migrants? Had our lack of linguistic competence in Farsi/Kurdish/Arabic cut us off from important information? Our research demonstrates that the explanation is more complicated than that: in spite of the fact that the interviewees were articulate about these problems, the conflicts were never played out in the open. Somehow, their shared new faith curbed potential confrontations. Methodologically considered, neither participant observation alone, nor isolated interviews, would have given us access to the complex interactions between the asylum seekers' and refugees' social worlds and experiences, and the way they interpreted their lives theologically.

The aim of this essay is two-fold. First, we want to understand why the Eucharist is able to curb social and ethnic conflicts. Second, we want to scrutinise how asylum seekers' and refugees' appropriation of the Eucharist affects the theology of the ELCD. The essay consists of three parts: First, we present our 'data' and focus on the tensions that the 'ordinary' meals in and around the Apostles' Church generated. Next, we account for the reconfiguration of the Christian Gospel, which we encountered in our interviews with the migrants. To give you a foretaste: according to our interviewees, Christ did not die for the sake of our sin, which constitutes the fulcrum of the Protestant, Lutheran Gospel, but to witness and prevent human suffering because of sin. These two sections will answer our first question. After that, we turn toward theory and discuss "How to Do Things with Rituals": how rituals may push and provoke changes in the worldview, in this case, a new theology.

Tensions at the Table

The Afghan Cook: A Request for Etiquette and Recognition

One of the first persons we interviewed was the Afghan man, who cooked for the asylum seekers and refugees when, after the Sunday service, this group came together for a Bible-study class. As typically fifty to eighty migrants would participate in the lunch after the class, the organization of the meal called for logistic and economic skills besides the need for professional cooking experience.[5] The Afghan cook has these skills. He grew up in Afghanistan, where he worked in a bakery during his adolescent years. For reasons unknown to us, he fled to Iran at the age of thirteen, where he lived illegally for twenty-seven years. In Iran, he ended up having a small shop with vegetables, in which he also sold salads and sandwiches. The income from the shop was enough to raise a family. He has an Iranian wife and a grown-up son and daughter. Whereas the daughter still lives with the

---

5.   During the spring of 2017, the congregation in the Apostles' Church replaced the migrants' Bible-study class with an open café. The aim of this change was to encourage the integration of the Danish and migrant members of the church. The study of the Bible is now one option among many other activities, including gardening and table football. The fact that the whole congregation now gathers after service implies that the dishes the Afghan cook must prepare have doubled.

mother back in Iran, the son has obtained residence permission in Germany. Both male members of the family have converted to Christianity. His wife approves of their conversion, but the female members of the family have not changed religion. He explains that his flight to Europe was due to the unbearable condition that illegal residents must tolerate in Iran; they have no legal rights. For example, since he did not exist as a legal person, he was not allowed to marry his wife. In addition, if subjected to injustice or even violence, he had nowhere to go with his complaints. But because the whole system benefits from this kind of quasi-official immigration, he did not expect any improvement in his situation.

The cook's story is typical for many uneducated asylum seekers who are not politically organized: frequently, the authorities reject applications for residence from this group. The circumstances around their flight are typically a mix of social, ethnic, and religious issues, none of which appears serious enough for the authorities to grant refugee status. Nevertheless, when one kind of oppression is added upon another, the situation ends up being weighty enough for the person to embark on a risky journey that will separate him (usually, it is a male) from family, history and country. Often the plan is that the family should follow, but in a safer manner, when the man has received permission to remain in the host country.

During the interview, the Afghan cook told us that he was happy to serve the church with his skills. He also conveyed a certain pride about his ability to cook for so many people. To him, cooking was his gift to the church and its congregation, as he put it, 'My way of serving Christ'. Nevertheless, he sometimes felt that the participants in the meals that he had prepared did not understand his efforts in this way. The cook described two situations in which he felt his work was unappreciated. The first related to a group of Afghan male adolescents. Occasionally, when he had prepared a meal for himself in the church, he invited a couple of these young men to share it. However, it left him angry when they just took his cooking for granted and did not even bother to do their own dishes. In another of our interviews, a young Iranian woman explained the Afghan boys' misbehaviour to us. Due to their hunger, the guys often disturbed the cook in the kitchen before the food was ready. In addition, they also messed up the line for the meal: 'They are too hungry to wait for the first serving and still too hungry to wait patiently for the second....So don't make the prayer before the meal too long', she joked. A middle-aged, Iranian, female interviewee also addressed the young men's inappropriate behaviour. The problem was, she explained, that young male asylum seekers had no experience with the cost-saving economy of poor people's kitchens: they did not know how to cook. In addition, they just wanted to live like Danish adolescents: they, too, go to McDonalds. But when an asylum seeker buys a Big Mac, he will not have money for the coming day's breakfast and lunch.

The cook also described his relationship with the Iranians: sometimes he felt they ignored and belittled him. This experience reminded him of his time in Iran, where he, as an illegal Afghan immigrant worker, had felt reduced to a non-person whose services the Iranians just took for granted.

Proustian Identity Formation: Staple Food and Memory

The staple food accompaniments to the Sunday lunch were the occasion of another set of ethnically related problems. We did not catch these tensions, nor were the ministers from the Apostles' Church aware of the conflicts and of the role they played in them. The problem was that we all tended to lump every person of Middle Eastern origin into one 'oriental' group. It was the same with the languages: tongues foreign to the European ear were, in spite of the differences, identified as Farsi. Accordingly, the Afghans, Iranians, Iraqis and Kurds within the congregation were all seen as belonging to 'the Farsi group'. For the same reason, all kinds of spicy food were enjoyed as variations of the same exotic curried dish. However, our interviews revealed that the group of asylum seekers and refugees consisted of more complex, and often minority ethnicities, such as Kurdish Iraqis and Iranians as well as Arab Iranians, groups whose mother tongue differed from Farsi and whose food habits varied from Iranian customs.

One of our interviewees was a Kurdish man who had been affiliated with the Apostles' Church for the past fifteen years. He had come to Denmark in the early 1990s as a refugee from Saddam Hussein's heavy attack on the Kurds in northern Iraq. As a response to the Kurds' national uprising after the war between Iraq and Iran, Saddam Hussein suppressed the 'rebels' in a brutal campaign conducted by the Iraqi Republican Guard. Thousands of Kurds died, and several Kurdish villages were obliterated. All this was part of our interviewee's history. When we asked him to describe the development that he had seen in and around the Apostles' Church during the past fifteen years, he asked us twice if we wanted an honest description. When confirmed, he explained that, personally, he felt that the Danish leaders tended to favour Iranians at the expense of Kurds and Afghans. He explained this situation by reference to the different national psyche that, according to him, characterized the various ethnic groups. Maybe it was only natural that the Iranians got more attention because, as he put it, 'They are beautiful and extroverted'. In contrast, he described the Kurds, Afghans, and Arabs as more introverted people: 'The wars have made us and the Afghans tougher, more introverted'. To him, the serving of rice at all meals was one of the ways in which the Iranians were favoured. In contrast, bread, which constituted the Kurdish people's most important staple food and which was an essential part of their culture, rarely accompanied the curry. When as a young adult, he had fled with his mother and siblings up into the mountains, the only food they carried with them was flour. As he explained to us, 'With water, a fire and the precious flour, you are able to survive'. Sense perceptions related to the production and consumption of bread—the smell of bread being baked, the sound of fresh bread being broken, the taste of the crust—carried his history and in a Proustian way activated his memory.

At the meals, a fried rice-cake, which some migrants broke and shared among themselves, had attracted our attention several times. Later we found out how the cook made it: while the rice was still steaming, he or she poured olive oil into the pot and the rice at the bottom fried into this crispy cake, which was called *tadig*. However, *tadig* was more than an appreciated delicacy. We saw how, as a kind of ethnic Eucharist, the sharing of *tadig* established an ethnic community within the migrant group. An assembly of Iranians was ritually separated out from the rest of the congregation. The *tadig* confirmed their identity by activating their cultural memory through the senses: the taste, the smell, and the crunchy character of the *tadig* reminded them of their unique background.

Whereas the serving of ordinary meals activated social and ethnic tensions and threatened to split the migrant community, their shared participation in the Eucharist apparently curbed these tensions. However, in order to understand how, we have to understand the migrants' version of the Gospel. A series of photos taken by another Afghan interviewee, a man, probably in his mid-twenties, shed light on this.

The Migrants' Gospel: Christ as a Witness of Human Suffering

In order to take his photos for the interview, this Afghan man had chosen a church other than the Apostles' Church, namely the Trinity Church in the centre of Copenhagen. Assisted by a friend, he had taken a series of symbolically loaded pictures of different parts of the interior of the church. In the photographs, he depicted himself interacting with the paintings, the altar, the interior architecture, and so on. Some of the photos show him in front of the altar. Imitating the minister's gestures of prayer, he stretches out his arms to the sides, with the effect that his body mirrors the crucified and the cross. For the interview, he had also brought a t-shirt that was stained with blood. We understood that the blood was his, but we do not know why he brought it for the interview. Since the memories invoked by the t-shirt made him feel very uncomfortable, we did not press him for knowledge about the specific situation that had generated the alleged violence. During the interview, he also, less dramatically, told us about how he often assisted the cook in the kitchen and helped doing the dishes. Jesus' sacrifice was an important motive for serving the community, because, as he explained, by doing this he 'served Jesus who sacrificed himself for our sake'. Reflecting on the crucified Christ, he explained that, to him, Christ was a witness of human suffering.

Our conversation with this Afghan man throws light on a tendency that we found in all the interviews: the parallel focus on Christ's sacrifice and their own serving. However, when speaking about Christ's suffering, they did not refer to the Apostles' Creed. Instead of belief in 'the forgiveness of sins', that is, Christ's vicarious punishment for human sins, they spoke about Christ's suffering as *witnessing* human suffering. When in his photos, the Afghan man imitated the minister's liturgy of prayer, he had Christ's crucifixion mirroring his own body. In this way, he demonstrated how Christ was a witness of his personal story. Moreover, in his theological reflections on the photographs, he exchanged God's forgiveness of human sins with human beings' obligation to stop the violence by leaving their evil thoughts under the covered space at the church door, which, as he also reminded us, was called the 'house of weapons' in Danish. Thus, it was Christ's suffering, not on behalf of sinful humanity, but as a witness of humanity's suffering because of sin that made the cooking of rice, dishwashing, and toilet cleaning into meaningful jobs.

Let us briefly return to the Afghan cook. In our interview with him, he explained how his current vulnerable situation, with several rejected applications for asylum, did not really matter to him. The place to which he primarily related was neither his former homeland(s), nor the country that refused his applications, but the utopian Kingdom of God: 'I feel that I have already received my residence permit by the Gospel and by converting to Christianity and God the almighty in heaven'. As a pledge of the coming Kingdom, his participation in Christ overruled national sentiments and affiliations. On the one hand, the meal he prepared represented his personal history; on the other hand, his new faith drowned out his ethnic sensibilities.

All this explains why participating in and assisting at the Eucharist had become such an important goal for the converts to obtain: when they consume the host, they are, together with every person participating in the ritual, incorporated into the body of Christ. As members of this congregational body, the converts feel an obligation "to take up their cross" and let their own life be an enactment of the(ir) Gospel. Consequently, the replacement of the bread with the printed wafer host appeared highly meaningful to the migrants: the Christological interpretation of the ritual mirrored the migrants' Gospel with its peculiar focus on Christ's witnessing function.

Stripped of any material reference to ethnic, staple food, the white, anonymous wafer had become a signifier with an open, arbitrary signified: the oblate may equally represent Danish or Kurdish bread or the Iranian *tadig* made of rice.[6] The Eucharist allowed the participants to interpret the wafer host according to their own chthonic food traditions, but also inspired them, when they hosted 'ordinary' meals, to offer their own ethnic food as spiritually motivated gifts for the congregation, as we saw in the case of the Afghan cook. Becoming a Christian does not supersede the migrants' ethnic identity, but their ethnicity is modified and reframed in light of their new faith and made instrumental to that. Thus, their new identity may be characterized as quasi-ethnic or hybrid: they have become Christian Kurds, Christian Iraqis etc. It was this double identity that simultaneously provoked the ethnic sensibilities and curbed potential ethnic conflicts.

How to Do Things with Rituals: Disrupting Protestant Lutheran Theology

In order to understand even better the role that the Eucharist played in the reconfiguration of the congregation's social space and in the reinterpretation of Protestant Lutheran theology, a glance at recent theories of ritual and performativity may be helpful.

The Play between Sameness and Difference in Ritual Theory

In our study, the use of Amy Hollywood's analysis 'Performativity, Citationality, Ritualization' (2006), in which she reviews contemporary theories of ritual in the light of Judith Butler's work on performativity, has proved fruitful. She links Catherine Bell's work on ritualization with the theories that informed *Gender Trouble* (1990) and revisits Frits Staal's and

---

6. In our analysis, we were inspired by the brilliant analysis of the host as sign in Catherine Gallagher and Stephen Greenblatt's 'The Wound in the Wall' from their book *Practicing New Historicism* (2001).

Talal Asad's studies on rituals with inspiration from *Bodies That Matter* (1993). Throughout her analysis, Hollywood focuses on the play between sameness and difference in the various theories. This peculiar perspective allows us to approach theories, which have often been seen as complete contrasts, as a dynamic continuum between these poles. Her work therefore offers us a complex approach that enables us to identify and understand opposing tendencies at work in our 'data'.

The thesis forwarded in Butler's *Gender Trouble* (1990) is well known: as phenomenon, gender comes into being through the social recognition of continuously *performed* bodily citations. In order to substantiate her claim, Butler had recourse to J. L. Austin's speech acts and Jacques Derrida's play with difference. It is the relationship between performativity and these theories that has relevance in our case. Whereas Austin was concerned to avoid 'misfiring' and therefore emphasized the contextual and intentional conditions that speech acts had to fulfil in order for the 'performative' to be decoded rightly, Derrida had pointed to the fact that as soon as these contextual preconditions were no longer present, the semantic flexibility involved in any (speech) act would once more be released. The first under-lined sameness, the other difference, yet the two agreed that the meaning of a (speech) act was determined by the context in which the act was embed-ded. Hollywood places Bell's theory of ritualization within this framework. When, according to Bell, we perceive a particular performance as a ritual, it is due to the intentional *difference* at play in the bodily citation. An example from our study will illustrate her point. The Eucharist is recognized as a ritual because at the same time as it mimics the ordinary meal, it also *differs* from everyday eating in significant ways. On the one hand, the eating is real: the bread or the host is ingested. On the other hand, the participants do not eat with the intention of satisfying our hunger; after all, the amount of food consumed is too small for that. Consequently, the intentionality of the act is experienced as being directed toward something else. However, the space that this displaced intentionality opens, is left for interpretation. The ritual is enriched with a new potential of meaning(s).

Whereas Butler in *Gender Trouble* had focused on the subject and its repertoire of performances, *Bodies That Matter* situated her work in a long tradition of scholarship influenced by Marcel Mauss' work on body tech-niques in which he emphasized the role of the social in identity formation. Above all, Mauss' analyses have inspired Pierre Bourdieu's concept of the *habitus* and Michel Foucault's reflections on subjectivity in terms of sub-jection and discipline. After all, it is the social recognition that determines which of the actualized potentials comes into 'being'. Two ritual theorists, in particular, should be linked with this tradition: Talal Asad with his return to medieval conceptions of the ritual in terms of rules and discipline discussed in 'Genealogy of the Concept of Ritual' (1993), and Frits Staal, who in his famous essay of the same name, speaks about 'The Meaninglessness of Ritual' (1979). According to these two scholars, the very performance of the ritual constitutes its 'meaning'. The 'significance' of ritual behaviour is bound to the social recognition of the correctness of the performance. Consequently, the ritual has no cognitive content; it is, as claimed by Staal, characterized by 'meaninglessness'.

Bell and Asad/Staal represent two different trajectories within ritual studies. Whereas Bell sees difference as the constitutive element in rituals, the Asad/Staal tradition claims that rituals are constituted by rules and repetition, in other words, by sameness. According to Bell, ritualization is an innovative and constructive enterprise capable of stimulating new meaning and of reconfiguring social structures. Conversely, Asad and Staal see ritual behaviour as a conservative activity: when the play between sameness and difference in the ritual is reduced to sameness, no (new) meaning is possible. Consequently, when participants in a particular performance emphasise rule-right repetition, the ritual tends to confirm the *status quo*. In spite of the fact that the two groups of theories emphasize different aspects of the ritual, most rituals will be located between these two poles in practice.

Revisiting the Eucharist: The Refugees' Other-wise Understanding

These theoretical reflections can help us understand and explain how the presence of new hosts and new participants at the Lord's Table reconfigured the Eucharist and disrupted Protestant Lutheran theology. Although nothing was changed in the prescribed liturgy: the words accorded with the Ordo and the traditional, printed wafer was used, the fact that it was no longer the Danish ministers alone who hosted the Eucharist, but a diversity of ethnicities and races, of males and females, of different ages, revitalized the ritual. The tipping of the balance between sameness (the Ordo) and difference (new hosts and new participants) in favour of the latter opened up the ritual and enriched it with meaning, or rather, potentials of meaning.

The lives of the newcomers in the congregation constitute the obvious context for an actualization of this potential. As demonstrated in the introduction, the church interior prompted migrants and Danes to mix at the Lord's Table. Inevitably, the proximity to a person, maybe the man or woman kneeling next to you, who is physically and psychologically marked by war or torture (as is the case of many refugees), will affect the interpretation of the ritual. Sin is moved away from the private space between the individual worshipper and God and placed in a global context where it represents the power structures that impede the flourishing of life. Apart from this pressing exposure of evil, members from the Danish part of the congregation are acquainted with the asylum seekers' and refugees' life stories because of their voluntary work or regular presence in the church. Thus, the Eucharist looked like the traditional ritual for the absolution of personal sin. Yet something very different took place. Through the consumption of the host with the print of the crucified Lord, the participants simultaneously incorporated Christ into their body and were incorporated into his body. In this way, they became bodily representations of, or in their own understanding, missionaries for, their version of the Gospel.

In the beginning of the chapter, we mentioned the two dominant tendencies in Danish theology and ecclesiology: the liberals, who gather around the creator God, and the more conservative, who invoke the Redeemer God and his Son. However, the refugees' theology/Christology does not fit into that scheme, but represents a third option. The refugees do not gather around the Lord's Table as perpetrators of sin in need of forgiveness, but as victims of sin or in solidarity with these victims. Their version of the history of God's involvement with the world also differs from the understanding of the majority church. The creation is not, as claimed by most Christian denominations, 'fallen'; instead, the will of the Creator has not yet come into being. Consequently, they enter the altar space as co-workers on this theo-political project.

In the introduction, we also mentioned the participation of Muslims at the Lord's Table in the Apostles' Church. Although they do not receive the elements of bread and wine, they come to the altar for the blessing and the experience of community. Here we face a difference between the ritual practice in the Apostles' Church and the performance of the Eucharist in many ELCD congregations, which do not welcome Muslim participation in the Eucharist. This difference also requires interpretation. To some politicians, and some officials in the asylum system, it appears as a kind of strategic mockery of the Christians' most valuable sacrament with the purpose of receiving a residence permit. However, a survey, which was carried out among the Farsi- and Kurdish-speaking part of the congregation in the Apostles' Church during the summer 2014, revealed a different interpretation.[7] The survey data indicated that Muslims and Christians worshipped

---

7.   Financed by the ELCD, Jonas Boendergaard carried out a questionnaire survey among the international participants in the Apostles' Church. Unfortunately, his survey is not published, but the results are accessible through the author and the Apostles' Church.

the same god. Consequently, if the Muslim migrants chose to be baptized, they did not convert from one god to another, but changed the way they worshipped and served the only God they recognised. According to their world view, when they entered the space around the altar in order to receive the divine blessing, it was a deeply meaningful act. In the long term, the migrants' other-wise understanding of the ritual may be seen as an invitation from 'below' to Christian theologians to reflect on the relationship between the religions.

As promised in the introduction, we return to the young Afghan man and his experience as a first time host. The grand old man of American anthropology, Marshall Sahlins, will help us to understand his emotional reaction.

Postscript: The Eucharist and Kinship Formation

'I felt so warm inside ...'
The young Afghan man, mentioned in the first epigraph,
about his experience as a first time host at the Eucharist.

In his 2013 book *What Kinship Is—And Is Not*, Marshall Sahlins reconsiders the concept of kinship in light of a century of anthropological research. He criticizes the prominence ascribed to consanguinity in former anthropological research on kinship. Once more, Western scholars had universalized a Western perspective: some anthropologists made the Western construction of kinship into an analytical category, which was then applied to different cultures' very different ways of establishing kinship. Instead, according to Sahlins, kinship is a way to express the experience of 'mutuality of being'. As Sahlins' approach to kinship is quite new, his thesis deserves to be quoted in full:

> In brief, the idea of kinship in question is "mutuality of being": people who are intrinsic to one another's existence—thus "mutual person(s)," "life itself," "intersubjective belongings," "transbodily being," and the like. I argue that "mutuality of being" will cover the variety of ethnographical documented ways that kinship is locally constituted whether by procreation, social construction, or some combination of these. Moreover, it will apply equally to interpersonal kinship relations, whether "consanguineal" or "affinal," as well as to group arrangements of descent. Finally, "mutuality of being" will logically motivate certain otherwise enigmatic effects of kinship bonds—of the kind often called "mystical"—whereby what one person does or suffers also happens to others. (Sahlins 2013: 3)

In every culture, this experience of mutuality tends to be hypostasized and deposited in a shared medium. In the monotheistic, Abrahamic religions (Judaism, Christianity and Islam), the medium is identified with the ancestor's semen: it is 'consanguineal'. However, a century of anthropological fieldwork has documented that other cultures project their experience of 'mutuality of being' onto a variety of media. It may rest with the sharing of food, the sharing of an environment (the soil), the sharing of spirit, of pain and so forth. As Sahlins explains,

> Mutuality in being has the virtue of describing the various means by which kinship may be constituted, whether natally or post-natally, from pure "biology"' to pure performance, and any combinations thereof ... however such consubstantiality is locally defined and established. Neither a universal nor an essential condition of kinship, common substance is better understood as a culturally relative hypostasis of common being. (Sahlins 2013: 28)

Sahlins also points to the Eucharist as a ritual that combines several of these consubstantial alternatives: at the Lord's Table we find the shared ancestor (Christ), the shared food (the wine and the bread), and the shared cosmos (the spirit). In addition, the very eating of the medium is an effective way of incorporating the 'transbodily being'. In our interviews, several asylum applicants added yet another consubstantial element to the Eucharist: shared pain or suffering. Although the official, dogmatic, confessional interpretation of the Eucharist links the ritual with the absolution of sin, from an anthropological point of view it is an extremely strong generator of kinship ties.

During spring 2017, we succeeded in getting an interview with the young Afghan man referred to in the epigraph that introduces the chapter. In 2014, we had not invited him for a photo-interview. Nevertheless, he figured prominently in the photographs taken by the other interviewees. We saw a picture of him serving at the Eucharist, which was taken shortly after he had been baptized. In some of the photos, he works: he sweeps the floor or is engaged in some other kind of maintenance job. In other snapshots, he is just hanging around, which is due to the fact that, during the summer 2014, he lived in the Apostles' Church. His applications for asylum had been rejected and, in this situation, he had chosen to go underground and disappear from the authorities. He was (and is) a young man who does not blow his own horn. Perhaps that explains why we did not seek him out for an interview. Nonetheless, his presence was (and is) strongly felt in the congregation, as the photos documented. Although he stayed underground for nearly three years, eventually the authorities caught him. Yet with the aid of lawyers volunteering their time, he managed to have his case reconsidered by the Refugee Appeals Board.

We talked to him a couple of days before the final processing of his case. In the interview, he told us about his childhood. He was orphaned early in his life, but an uncle had accepted him into his household. However, he did not live with the family, but served it with his work. When his cousins went to school, he stayed at home and worked in the field, with the animals, and in the house. Consequently, he had never learned to read and write. To avoid daily beatings, he ran away at the age of ten and followed an older boy to Iran. There he worked as car mechanic in a small workshop for a couple of years before he accompanied some other migrants who left Iran for Europe.[8] The adequate category, which should be applied to his history, is child slavery. When he described his happiness and the warmth that he felt inside when hosting the Eucharist, we suggest that it is understood in the light of Sahlins' analysis of the Eucharist: In this particular congregation, he had found a family.

References

Armour, Ellen T., and Susan M. St. Ville (2006), *Bodily Citations: Judith Butler and Religion.* New York: Columbia University Press.
https://doi.org/10.1163/156852779X00244.

Asad, Talal (1993), *Genealogies of Religion: Discipline and Reasons of Power in Christianity and Islam.* Baltimore: Johns Hopkins University Press.
https://doi.org/10.1017/s0020743800061195.

Bell, Catherine (2009) [1992], *Ritual Theory, Ritual Practice.* Oxford: Oxford University Press.

Boendergaard, Jonas (2014), 'Anonymous Survey among Farsi- & Kurdish-speaking Refugees in Apostelkirken International (AI). Sunday the 11th of May 2014'. Unpublished.

Buch-Hansen, Gitte (2018), 'Converting Refugees and the(ir) Gospel: Exegetical Reflections on Refugees' Encounter with Denmark and with the Lutheran Church', in Jesper Høgenhaven, Jesper Tang Nielsen, and Heike Omerzu, eds., *Rewriting and Reception in and of the Bible.* Tubingen: Mohr Sierbeck.
https://doi.org/10.1628/978-3-16-155439-1.

8.   Skilled as a mechanic in her early career, the author of this article confirms that the young man's knowledge of various welding techniques was sound.

Buch-Hansen, Gitte, Marlene Ringgaard Lorensen, and Kirsten Donskov Felter (2015), 'Ethnographic Ecclesiology and the Challenges of Scholarly Situatedness', *De Gruyter Open Theology*, 220–244. https://doi.org/10.1515/opth-2015-0009.

Butler, Judith (1993), *Bodies That Matter: On the Discursive Limits of 'Sex'*. New York: Routledge.

Butler, Judith (1990), *Gender Trouble: Feminism and the Subversion of Identity*. New York: Routledge.

Gallagher, Catherine, and Stephen Greenblatt (2001), *Practicing New Historicism* Chicago: University of Chicago Press. https://doi.org/10.1162/00221950152103937.

Høgenhaven, Jesper, Jesper T. Nielsen, and Heike Omerzu (2018), *Rewriting and Reception in and of the Bible: Festschrift Mogens Müller*. Tübingen: Mohr Siebeck.

Hollywood, Amy (2006), 'Performativity, Citationality, Ritualization', in Ellen T. Armour and Susan M. St. Ville, eds. *Bodily Citations: Religion and Judith Butler*. New York: Columbia University Press, 252–275.

Sahlins, Marshall (2013), *What Kinship Is—And Is Not*. Chicago: University of Chicago Press.

Staal, Frits (1979), 'The Meaninglessness of Ritual'. *Numen*, 26/1, 2–22.

About the Author

Gitte Buch-Hansen is associate professor in biblical studies, the Faculty of Theology, Copenhagen University. In 2013–2016, she participated in the project Reassembling Democracy: Ritual as Cultural Resource. Since 2014, she has been engaged in fieldwork among migrants in Copenhagen who, as part of their application for asylum, have converted from Islam to Christianity. Her research focuses on the way that conversion affects the applicants' life stories and how the presence of refugees influences the church in Denmark and its congregations. In addition, she brings her work among contemporary migrants back to the formative phase of Christianity, where it sheds light on previously unnoticed aspects with regard to migration and conversion. She has published several articles in this field—e.g. 'Listening to the Voices: Refugees as co-Authors of Practical Theology' (with Marlene Ringgaard Lorensen), *Practical Theology*, 11/1 (2018) and "Converting Refugees and The(ir) Gospel: Exegetical Reflections on Refugees' Encounter with Denmark and with the Lutheran Church" in *Rewriting and Reception in and of the Bible* (2017).

Part 3
Performances

6. Dances of Self-Development as a Resource for Participatory Democracy

Michael Houseman and Marie Mazzella di Bosco

'One solution may lie in rituals' (Polletta 2002:224)

This article explores the political dimensions of collective dance practices undertaken largely in the spirit of self-discovery and personal transformation: 5 Rhythms, Movement Medicine, Biodanza, Life Art Process, Sacred Circle Dance, and others. Sometimes glossed as 'ecstatic', 'spiritual', or 'free' dance, activities such as these first appeared in the 1960s, and have expanded over the last few decades to become a regular feature of most major European and American cities. They typically take the form of weekly two-hour sessions run by an 'instructor' or 'facilitator'. A session, costing 15 to 20 euros, brings together between fifteen and fifty participants, predominantly middle-class Caucasians, three-fourths of whom are women, and whose average age is around forty (very few participants are under twenty-five).

These 'focused gatherings' (Goffman 1961) are neither therapy sessions, esoteric apprenticeships, dance classes, nor dance parties. As their practitioners often insist, while they may prove therapeutic, they are not therapy; they do not claim to be remedial treatments for psychological or physical disorders. At the same time, as practices immediately accessible to all, requiring little effort or commitment (regular participation, while encouraged, is not a prerequisite), they are not esoteric, initiation-based disciplines. Finally, in the course of these sessions, dance is treated less as an end in itself than as a means for attaining special, out-of-the-ordinary outcomes related to participants' personal development and self-realization. As such, these activities can be distinguished both from those aimed at developing proficiencies in dance (almost none of the participants are trained dancers), and from recreational or social dancing undertaken within the context of mundane concerns such as seduction, companionship, physical fitness, and so forth.

According to the flyers, websites, and books that promote them, these practices allow participants to 'rediscover' their innate yet heretofore unrealized capacities for 'spontaneity', 'creativity', and 'authenticity'. They are 'an invitation to encounter and express one's personal strength', a way to find 'a state of being present to oneself', to 'touch and taste one's Being through dance', to 'find and experience one's deepest self', to 'explore the wondrous and magical dimensions that lie within each of us'. These activities are thus explicitly oriented towards individual self-discovery and personal fulfilment. They number among the wide array of practices consistent with one of the hallmark expectations of Western individualism: the deliberate construction of the self (Giddens 1991, Taylor 2007, Le Bart 2008 among others). As such, collective dancing, along with other contemporary 'alternative' initiatives, can readily be seen through the prism of individualistic consumerism in which 'seekers' (Heelas 1996) 'pick-and-mix' (Hamilton 2000) from among a variety of commoditized offers (the 'spiritual supermarket') in keeping with what are presumed to be their personal needs and desires (cf. Luckmann 1996, Van Hove 1999, Roof 1999). Now, this may be true up to a point, but as has been argued for shopping (Miller 1998), 'foodies' (de Solier 2013), personal development books (Marquis 2014), and self-spirituality generally (Aupers and Houtman 2013), it is far from the whole story.

Discourse relating to these practices, as well as the dance sessions themselves, play up self-discovery, but they also emphasize mutual respect, collective sentiment, and the ideal of public commitment to a larger social and environmental assemblage. Hence the recurrent motif of the three-fold 'connection' these activities are presumed to promote: to oneself, to others (or 'the group') and to 'the world' (or to 'nature' or 'the environment'). Dance sessions often enact these connections, not only during short-term partnerships and the studied expressions of gratitude that follow, but also in certain patterns of movement as when the partners of randomly formed couples are invited to divide themselves into 'dancers' and 'witnesses'. The latter form a circle surrounding their dancing partners to whom they 'bring support and deep attention', before thoughtfully (but silently) thanking each other and exchanging roles. The same holds true for relationship to the group. Thus, persons who, because they are fearful, upset or just tired, prefer to stop dancing for a while, move to the side but are asked not to cut themselves off from the group. In the same vein is one 5 Rhythms instructor's firm admonition upon seeing people dancing by themselves in spite of her repeated collective invitations to the contrary: 'When I suggest dance movements involving two, three or more people, this is never an obligation! There are moments when one needs to be alone. However, the idea in these sessions is that everyone should bring something to the community. If you really don't want to do this, there are plenty of other types of dances elsewhere' (all translations from the French are ours). There is indeed a subtle equilibrium to be found during these sessions between personal autonomy on the one hand and a feeling of responsibility towards those present and the community at large on the other. The day following the November 2015 terrorist attacks in Paris, a 5 Rhythms facilitator decided to maintain the scheduled session in order to 'put movement and life back into everyone, after the shock that froze us all'. Many people came, and one participant's testimony attests to this collective bond: 'I didn't really feel like dancing, but it was important to be here, together, with you all.' During the session, participants lit candles which they placed on an improvised shrine; at the end, they were invited to bring them to the nearby Place de la République 'to share our inner peace with the world'.

Also relevant is the prevalence of participants working in care-centred, other-oriented professions. In several 5 Rhythms and Movement Medicine groups attended over a two-year period, around one quarter of the most assiduous dancers were employed in the fields of psychology and health, and another quarter in that of education. A third quarter worked in various artistic professions, and a final quarter had a wide variety of occupations (engineers, office workers, etc.). Some participants said they had recently undergone training to look for new jobs in the fields of care or education. However, generally speaking, their professional orientations predated their involvement in these practices, and cannot be considered to have derived from them. Yet, dancing together has the enhancing effect of bringing together people with different but related social profiles, skills, and interests so as to create a loose, yet coherent network of altruistically oriented 'consequential strangers' (Fingerman 2009). At times, such as in the wake of the 2015 terrorist killings and the *Je suis Charlie* march in reaction to them, this complicity can assume a more political tone. In one Biodanza group, several participants who were schoolteachers, disoriented by the way their more disadvantaged students refused to be identified with Charlie, stressed how important it is to take a balanced ethical stance, and 'to provide young people with the means to think and feel with greater stability and security, so that they can express themselves without resorting to violence'. In another group, one participant suggested that 'We are all Charlie, but we are also all terrorists', and that 'we have to find the terrorist in each of us to be able to face the situation and act with wisdom'.

Finally, many participants are involved in one or more projects or associations that invest the public sphere in ways that resonate with what are usually recognized as 'democratic', anti-totalitarian (Arendt 1951) values: personal agency, pluralism, collective solidarity, social activism. In one 5 Rhythms group, for example, Nicole launched a 'democratic school', Jeanne was developing permaculture in Paris, and Julie, a professional photographer, had recently returned from a project in Africa combining photography and dance therapy to help abused women. Moreover, instructors regularly undertake initiatives that aim to take the restorative benefits of their practice beyond the private dance floor: one facilitator organized Biodanza sessions on the Place de la République during the *Nuit Debout* movement in Paris, a 5 Rhythms teacher is planning to set up dance sessions in a refugee camp in the Paris suburbs, while several other instructors have organized sessions to raise funds for the Red Cross, or for Standing Rock.

In many respects, then, the values voiced and acted out during dance sessions, as well as the professional and personal commitments of practitioners, suggest that these practices are not reducible to the consumption of a resource for individual self-fulfilment. They also mobilize a benevolent, negotiated openness to others, a feeling of personal responsibility towards the group, and an admittedly diffuse concern for broader issues. There is indeed general agreement among dance practitioners that one's personal development can better enable one to bring about change in the world.

At the same time, however, these practices are not organized according to democratic principles. Decision-making and conflict resolution, for example, remains the province of the instructor or facilitator alone. Moreover, the group's activities are not in themselves of a political nature. During two-hour weekly sessions, what participants mostly do is dance to music without speaking. In some cases (such as Biodanza), they are invited to undertake a series of choreographic 'propositions': dancing in a circle, walking hand in hand, coordinating one's movements with one or more others, etc. In most cases, however, dancers are encouraged to move about freely, drawing inspiration from the music's changing rhythms and tonalities, from each other, and from the leader's occasional, somewhat enigmatic cues: 'feel the energy rising through your body', 'find a movement you can trust and follow it', 'let go', 'that's right', etc. Although each session is a distinct, deliberately orchestrated whole, it usually starts off with slow, flowing music that becomes progressively faster and more rhythmical, reaching a plateau of intensity before slowing down and tapering off towards the end. In principle, each participant dances alone, albeit in the company of others. However, following the leader's prompts or on their own initiative, participants often enter into short-term dance partnerships, seeking to coordinate their movements playfully or with impassioned diligence. After having danced (or in some cases before dancing), all are invited to form a circle holding hands and, if they wish, to 'share something with the group'. While participants may evoke public events or episodes from their personal lives at this time, they mostly voice their positive feelings towards the practice itself and towards the group.

How should such practices be understood politically? What relationship, if any, do they have to participatory democracy? They are neither 'pre-political' in the usual (Aristotelian) sense, nor can they be construed as 'infra-political' modes of informal resistance (Scott 1990) or protest (Marche 2012). Like many other 'alternative' or 'spiritual' practices, they are not instances of political activism in and of themselves, yet they call into play moral and social values that are consonant with the principles that democratically inspired political initiatives seek to put into effect. We propose to understand these practices as ritual activities that can be related to the recent restructuring of political activism in an increasingly decentralized public domain. The 1960s saw the emergence of new forms of activism that are more horizontally organized, more mobile, and less personally encompassing than traditional political associations such as parties, trade unions, or institutionalized interest groups. They favour a more bottom-up, looser, individual-based type of democratic engagement in which personal networks momentarily coalesce around particular events. Collective dance practices like 5 Rhythms, Biodanza, Movement Medicine and the like, we suggest, involve participants in extra-ordinary yet lived-through situations that enact a special mode of sociability, many aspects of which are immediately relevant to the functioning of social movements based on participatory democratic principles. By affording participants with 'privileged' experiences in which individual autonomy and collective solidarity are made interdependent, these practices can be a resource for democratic commitment in the political sphere.

A first section describes the individual engagement, interpersonal encounters, and conviviality characteristic of these collective dances. We then look at attendance rates and the way individuals participate in these practices. Finally, we consider the role collective dancing might play in participants' political lives.

A Close Familiarity with Strangers

We have described elsewhere how these dance practices progressively shape participants' experience (Houseman, Mazzella di Bosco, and Thibaut 2016; Houseman in press). Suffice to say here that, guided by music, by ambient sensory cues (soft lighting, the use of incense, loose garments, the presence of altar-like installations, etc.), by the instructor's directives, and by fellow dancers' behaviour, participants continually oscillate between two experiential poles. On the one hand, much of the time, they are made acutely aware of their deliberate efforts to move 'spontaneously', to interact 'authentically' with others, and to explore, emotionally and physically, what this might concretely entail. On the other hand, these on-going efforts are punctuated by episodes of 'letting-go' in which their movements and those of others seem to come together in a coherent, flowing whole. In the course of this process, participants regularly experience powerful moments of bodily presence and emotional intimacy. Attitudes and feelings presumed to be habitually kept in check can be expressed in outpourings of tears, screams or laughter, in a sudden rush of deep anger, in wild, sensual or bizarre facial expressions. This is what Frederic, a regular dancer, calls the 'somewhat crazy side' of these practices: 'free movement is a bit like a walk into madness… letting our emotions go, letting the madness overcome us! But this is frightening! People are afraid they'll break down if they let go.'

The sought-after sensations of physical and affective 'flow' (Csikszentmihalyi 1990) that make these sessions so worthwhile can come about during solitary dance, as when participants are transported by the particularly fluid, self-evident quality of their own movements. At such times, fatigue and self-consciousness give way to the excitement of seemingly unlimited expressive freedom. However, as dancers readily attest, these 'moments of grace' often blossom while dancing with others. Philippe, for example, recalls 'a dance together with another dancer when I felt like we were communicating telepathically, without any effort. This was like… the music is great, my partner can hear what I'm doing, I hear what she's doing, and we are able to create things without touching each other, fully synchronous, extraordinarily beautiful… . This really was a state of communion with someone else, and with dance, all together.'

Such feelings of exalted intimacy also arise with respect to the group of dancers as a whole, bringing about a sensation of being part of an organic, dynamic community composed of a multiplicity of independent yet closely connected cells. 'The group' is often movingly thanked and affectionately acknowledged during talking circles, and Biodanza facilitators, for example, often insist on how much 'the group' and 'finding one's place in it', contributes to a 'deepening of the experience' their practice affords. The quality of 'the group', along with the nature of the venue and the instructor's personality (her 'specific energy' or 'musical universe'), is among the top three or four reasons participants give for choosing one session over another. Philippe, for example, admitted he kept returning to one instructor's weekly sessions in spite of being somewhat unsatisfied with her, so as to continue dancing 'with the people there'. As we will see further on, 'the group' in question is not a closed, fixed set of individuals; newcomers are always present, and from one session to the next even the core of regular attendees is never exactly the same. However, one of the instructor's responsibilities is to instil this sense of heartfelt community in spite of the gathering's ever-changing composition. Facilitators who are most appreciated are those whose manner of guiding, and whose musical choices and choreographic proposals do this best. Such community-building proposals include various (slow or fast) circle dances, figures in which participants cross all together from one side of the room to the other, and ever more inclusive progressions. In the latter, the instructor, for example, may ask everyone to find a partner, 'no matter who, the one who's nearer from you', and to 'present yourself to them through your dance', and 'surprise them with your feet'. After a minute, participants are told that 'the group of two joins another group of two', and 'all four begin to create another dance', 'surprising each other with their knees'. After a short while, 'four and four make eight' and 'create a new dance together', then 'eight and eight make sixteen', and so on until the entire assembly has been gathered into a single circle of dancers. The instructor then invites everyone to move freely within and around the group, to cross empty spaces, to weave in and out, to come closer and then go further away, etc. The result is a flowing, playful circulation of all in a spirit of ostentatiously shared jubilation. Smiling dancers seek eye-contact with others as they lightly touch hands or shoulders in passing, demonstrating both their affectionate attentiveness towards each other and their sensitivity to the overall patterning of their shared dance.

One might expect experiences and behaviours such as these to occur in more private settings, with family members, lovers, or close friends. However, it is remarkable that those with whom participants have these exceptional encounters are generally distant acquaintances, sometimes even complete strangers. There are of course exceptions to this. Some participants know each other for having undertaken training workshops together. Others, having danced in the same groups for years, have become friends and see each other outside the dance context. But this is not the norm, and such 'extramural' relationships are rarely linked to particularly intense dance interactions. Indeed, it is typically with people they are not ordinarily close to that participants feel free to experience powerful emotions and/or familiar connection during these dance practices. There is thus a surprising discrepancy between the intense intimacy characteristic of the experiences practitioners share while dancing, and the distance they maintain towards each other once dancing is over.

Many participants assume, or at least hope that their daily lives will be affected by the experiences they have while dancing: a new-found joy in the expressive capacities of one's body, an heretofore unrealized aptitude for deep and open engagement with others, the comforting force of feeling one-self to be an active part of a larger, supportive community. However, they are fully aware that the sociality they engage in while dancing is a special one, not to be confused with that of everyday interaction. Thus, while some more regular participants may go out for a drink or a meal together after a session, such gatherings are short-lived, 'the group' ceasing to exist beyond the bounds of the dance itself. This also appears to be the rule regarding danced encounters. Sophie, for example, says that dancing has taught her to stay true to herself while opening up to another person, so as to genuinely take him or her into account. However, she sees a real difference between the relationships she has with fellow practitioners during dance sessions and those she has with them outside of sessions. While dancing, she can feel 'moments of profound connection with other dancers, moments which have a very distinctive consistency and depth ... but after the dance session, if I try to speak and socialise with the persons concerned, it's as if everything has flattened out, the magic is lost'. Many others attest to this disparity. Lisa, for example, says that she has been disappointed several times after having met dancers outside of sessions: 'it was weird, we were awkward with each other....When you dance with people, you know, you are able to meet up with them on a definitely other, higher, level. While dancing with someone, you get an idea about him or her, but then, outside, it's as if we suddenly don't speak the same language anymore! In the end, I think that maybe, while dancing, you get to know him or her better than in everyday life'. Eric admits to clearly separating these two relational registers: 'the dance' entailing encounters that go no further than the sessions themselves on one side, all his other relationships on the other. He does not go dancing to meet new friends or possible lovers for example. As he explains: 'If there's one thing I truly love [in these practices], it's the intensity of the encounter, even when it's brief. These moments are precious. For me, it's beautiful when something like that happens even if we never see each other again. There is beauty in this fleeting, ephemeral, encounter'.

The characteristic sociability of these practices can be qualified as one of 'distanced intimacy' (Houseman in press) in two related ways. First, as the above quotations indicate, participants are fully conscious that the sentiments and interactions that occur while dancing are at a remove from those of everyday intercourse. It is clear for all concerned that the aim of these practices—whose quality is often explicitly appraised, sometimes critically—is not to encroach upon participants' private lives. Rather, it is to provide them with enjoyable, well-delineated experiences that can act as sources of inspiration in their everyday worlds. Second, while participants may momentarily be carried away by the intensity of their emotions or the 'flow' of the dance, they are constantly incited to be self-conscious observers of their own feelings and behaviour. Their exceptional dance floor experiences thus readily become the object of reflexive scrutiny. As previously mentioned, sensations of awkwardness, weariness or annoyance continually rise to the surface of dancers' awareness, resulting in doubts and confusion, as the following excerpt from our (M. Mazzella di Bosco) field notes attests:

> After two or three partnerships, we are invited to 'circulate through the entire space and share this dance with the group', to 'present ourselves to others, to say who we are, through our dance'. While trying to discover how to do this, I can't help thinking that if we are supposed to dance to present ourselves, we should also be paying attention to others' presentations and welcome them. So, I should also be a person who looks at a person who is presenting. But I can't do both at the same time, so what should I do? All these questions keep turning in my head the whole time.

Such a reflexive attitude is further encouraged by instructors' expectations that dancers circulate to form partnerships with people they are not familiar with. One Movement Medicine teacher always ends his sessions by inviting participants to 'hug at least one person you don't know', and Biodanza facilitators often explain how a wide variety of partnerships, in causing practitioners to negotiate and explore new ways of feeling and interacting, lets them better experience what they are capable of. Indeed, this type of self-consciousness can also have a more positive side, as Gilles' account suggests:

> For me, these dance workshops are experimental laboratories. The dance becomes interesting for me when I somehow add a consciousness

of the energy involved, when I can feel not only what is happening
within me, but also what is happening within the other in front of me,
and what is happening in the interaction between others and myself, on
a conscious *and* unconscious level. That is, when I begin to play with
the energy in a certain way, I can *see* how the others around react, and
when there is like a delicate attunement of the other's movement... I
can feel when the unconscious or the body of the other has sensed that
something is happening, even if the person in question is not fully conscious of it. And for me this is interesting to observe.

One consequence of the distancing these practices put into effect, and
the ongoing negotiations with oneself and with others it implies, is a strong
emphasis on participants' individual selves. Personal autonomy, and respect
for the personal autonomy of others, is one of the basic values these practices
enact. This applies especially to interactions between dancers. 'Respect others as well as yourself', for example, is one of the 'three rules' of Biodanza
that are repeated at the start of almost every session (the others are 'enjoy
yourself' and 'no speaking'). But it is also made manifest during choreographic proposals involving the entire group. It often happens that a number
of participants remain at odds with the intense communal connection they
bring about. While almost everyone is sharing a complexly coordinated,
joyous dance, one person, for example, might be moving in a subdued, self-
absorbed manner off to the side, another might run through the room at full
speed, while still another might be sitting on the ground in the middle of it
all. No one seems overly concerned about this, although there are limits to
what is felt to be acceptable. In general, dancers adapt their movements so
as to integrate these individuals who move at their own rhythm, and who
sometimes explain afterwards that they needed to 'live through the moment
by themselves before coming back to the group'. In this way, individual
disparities are demonstrated and integrated into the whole. Indeed, one of
the striking aspects of these practices is the degree to which personal specificity is accentuated, not only in instructors' discourse and in participants'
movements, attitudes and interactive styles, but also, for example, in the
weight given to the use of personal names and individual gestures during
talking circles. This ideal of personal independence within the context of
a larger, well-disposed and supportive community, and the creative heterogeneity it fosters is not always achieved. However, it comes out clearly in
the two reasons Eric gives to explain his passionate participation in these
practices: first, there is 'a great and unconditional respect for people, for
everyone', and second, as a result, there is 'an unparalleled level of freedom

and therefore a great, great, diversity'. After a 'magical' session, he posted the following, telling message on the Parisian dancers' Facebook page:

> I believe that many of us do 5 Rhythms, Movement Medicine or Open Floor just like these sticks [he has just described an altar-like installation in which four sticks are arranged so that they point out in several directions from a common centre]: building on these dances' universe to open up to the world and bring something special to it. [The dance floor] is a microcosm where we can find freedom, tolerance, individuality, encounters, sensuality, dynamism, savageness, strength, light, tears, laughter, loneliness, attentiveness, intimacy and oneself.

The aim of these practices is less to promote authentic, heart-felt relationships between participants or with the group as a whole, than to provide dancers with memorable, embodied experiences of what such interpersonal and collective connections might be. Participants are incited to explore ways of acting and feeling that these relationships are presumed to imply: spontaneity, self-respect, adaptability, responsibility, openness to others, trust, collective engagement, etc. By enacting these qualities through their movements and interactions they demonstrate, to themselves and to others, their heretofore-unrealized capacity for entertaining relations of this nature. It is this newly revealed personal potential that they are then expected to put into practice in their daily lives. In this respect, the music, the instructor's directives, one's own bodily sensations, and interactions with fellow dancers and with the group can be understood as so many resources participants draw upon in the service of their personal 'development'.

In principle, then, the exceptional experiences these practices provide are destined to be 'disembedded' (Giddens 1991) from their immediate social context—the dance floor and relationships with fellow dancers—to be applied elsewhere. Practitioners' ways of feeling and (inter)acting during dance sessions can thereby become a resource for other, more everyday situations. This transposition is made possible by the distinctive sociality these practices entail, in which feelings and (inter)actions are intimate, intense, and embodied, yet at the same time transitory, sharply circumscribed, and reflexively distanced. However, it is worth stressing that the out-of-the-ordinary, somewhat ambivalent sociability characteristic of these practices has two complementary entailments. 5 Rhythms, Biodanza, Movement Medicine and the like enable dancers to experience the ongoing, purposeful production of their individual 'selves'. At the same time, participants also experience close, positive interactions with ostensibly independent, self-directed persons like themselves who, together, compose a caring, supportive

collective. Indeed, within the context of the distanced intimacy these practices put into effect, personal specificity, social relationship and group membership are often felt to become reconciled in ways that routine interaction
rarely allows. Actively partaking in exceptional situations in which affectionate familiarity and personal independence are deemed mutually reinforcing, participants can feel free to indulge in the heady joys of what might
be called 'collective individualism', that is, of being autonomous together.

A Distributed Mode of Participation

We have argued that these collective dances are organized in such a way
that assumes a systematic complementarity between individual freedom and
diversity on the one hand, and collective participation and commitment on
the other. A similar complementarity applies to the strikingly diffuse, distributed patterns in which dancers take part in these practices.

A remarkable feature of these dances is that continued participation does
not seem to favour assiduous attendance to the exclusion of other pastimes,
but exactly the opposite. Most participants become involved in 5 Rhythms,
Movement Medicine, or Biodanza for relatively short periods of time, generally no more than several years, before moving on to other things; most
participants are also simultaneously engaged in a variety of other activities,
often in the fields of personal development and contemporary spirituality[1].
Louise, for instance, experimented with different types of (contemporary,
African or Latin) dance but which she considered too constraining; when,
following a friend's recommendation, she tried 5 Rhythms, she felt she had
'found something'. While attending 5 Rhythms classes, she tried Biodanza
once, but 'was not convinced', and began Contact Improvisation. Now, she
occasionally practices 5 Rhythms and Contact Improvisation, but also goes
to meditation classes, belongs to a 'clown-theatre', and regularly swims and
runs; she is interested in 'inner child therapy', and is an active member of a
support group for women who have been victims of violence. Nelly also tried
out many bodily practices when younger (ballet, karate, surfing, salsa, etc.),
but 'was never completely satisfied'. Her discovery of Authentic Movement

---

1   This has also been pointed out in connection with other 'alternative' spiritual practices such as neo-shamanist workshops (Lombardi 2016), New Age style
Afro-Brazilian spirit cults (Teisenhoffer 2015), and local New Age or contemporary
Pagan 'scenes' (e.g. Prince and Riches 2000, Wood 2007); see also Corrywright
2003 on 'webs of practice').

was a 'revelation' through which she came to know Circle Dancing and Dances of Universal Peace where she met a Movement Medicine teacher. She started practicing Movement Medicine, and then 5 Rhythms. In parallel, she explored Chinese body practices such as Tai Chi and Qi Gong, and has become a certified teacher of these techniques. She also belongs to a women's circle, practices meditation 'of the Full Moon', and at the time of the interview, was about to begin Fasciatherapy and Sensory Movement. Philippe, after practicing martial arts for years, tried Malkowski Free Dance on a friend's advice. Concomitantly, he began attending Mindfulness Based Stress Reduction (MBSR) meditation classes, where a fellow participant told him about 5 Rhythms sessions which, like Louise and many others, he found to be 'a revelation and real liberation'. At present, in addition to 5 Rhythms, he occasionally attends Movement Medicine sessions, Contact Improvisation classes, and keeps doing MBSR meditation 'because they are complementary'. Some dancers are also (often unpaid) teachers of other somatic or self-development techniques. Clarisse, for example, is a yoga instructor, while Daphné, once her working day as a psychoanalyst is over, teaches Mindfulness Meditation, and so forth. Finally, because it is so difficult to earn a living as a free dance instructor or Biodanza facilitator, almost all of them, if not fully employed elsewhere, also conduct a variety of other self-discovery initiatives. Given this diversity, it would be misleading to think of practices such as these as analogous to religious sects or cults. While it is extremely difficult to evaluate their healing or transformative effects, one consequence they do seem to have is to encourage participants to explore a wide range of other, comparable activities.

To the extent that individuals' participation is generally distributed over an array of related practices, sequentially and/or simultaneously, they partake in any given practice in a markedly diffuse fashion. Attendance patterns reflect this. Consider the somewhat extreme case of Biodanza in which regular attendance with the same small group of practitioners is strongly and explicitly encouraged. Figure 1 provides attendance data for two Biodanza groups over a six month period (from mid-September 2014 to the end March 2015): 17 sessions (out of a total of 23) for Pat's group which averaged 13 participants per session, and 22 sessions (out of 27) for Toni's group which averaged 20 participants per session (participants are ordered vertically and sessions horizontally). Although both groups were open to persons discovering this practice for the first time, they also included a number of experienced practitioners. Among them, five persons who regularly attended Pat's sessions had recently started a (three-year) training programme to become facilitators themselves. The presence of accomplished practitioners was even more pronounced in Toni's group which included half a dozen dancers who had just finished their training together. Although the activities of both groups were organized according to the same principles, the way people talked, moved, and related to each other was quite different, reflecting the personality of their respective leaders. Pat's sessions tended to be more easy-going yet formal and fairly cerebral, whereas Toni's, perhaps because the group was larger and included more people who had known each other for a longer time, were warmer and more emotionally expressive, but also more confrontational. One person who had attended both groups described the first as 'aerial' and the second as 'earthy', adding that she found the latter more challenging but that it allowed her to 'explore herself more deeply'.

In spite of the differences between the two groups, their attendance patterns are remarkably similar. In both cases, four types of participants have been distinguished: (1) 'regulars' who attended at least half of the sessions, (2) 'occasionals' who attended less than half but who were intermittently present during the period concerned, (3) 'transients' who attended several sessions, either consecutively or not, and then stopped coming, and (4) 'one-timers' who attended only once. Persons belonging to the first two categories saw themselves and were seen by others as being committed to the shared practice of Biodanza and to the group itself, this being especially the case of 'regulars' who, when unable to attend, usually phoned or sent an SMS accounting for their absence to the facilitator (who subsequently relayed the message to the other participants during talking circles). On the other hand, attendees of the two latter types, especially 'one-timers', were more curious visitors than anything else (although accomplished practitioners passing through have been included in this category as well). Inspired by Internet sites or word of mouth, or accompanying more regular practitioners, they came to give Biodanza a try, deciding that it was not for them after several or just one session.

In both groups, the core of 'regulars', persons who attended at least half the sessions, was surprisingly small: 15.5 per cent of all participants in Pat's group, 25.4 per cent in Toni's. 'Regulars' and 'occasionals' together, that is, more or less 'committed' dancers, make up less than half the total number of participants: a mere 24.1 per cent in Pat's case and 44.8 per cent in Toni's. In short, the overwhelming majority of dancers were occasional participants at best. Most attended either several sessions or a single session before moving on. In 5 Rhythms and Movement Medicine groups, which assemble a larger number of people (forty on average, with a maximum of eighty) and in which participation is both more diverse and more open-ended, the proportion of first-timers per session was even higher that for Biodanza: 13 per

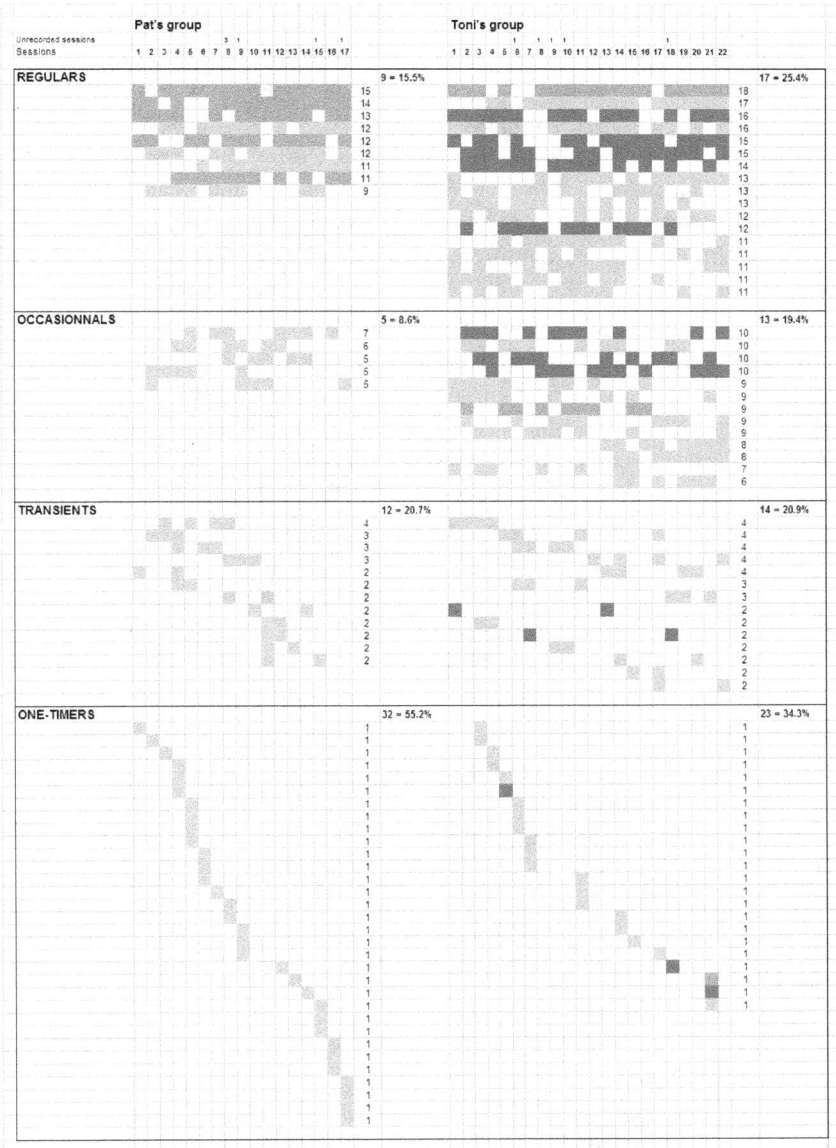

= Participant = Participant in training = Participant having finished training

Figure 1.

cent on average, with a maximum of 22 per cent (based on 38 sessions over a six-month period). However, for all practices, because committed dancers ('regulars' plus 'occasionals') represent the majority of participants for any given session, this overall predominance of 'transients' and 'one-timers' goes largely unnoticed. While 'transients' and 'one-timers' see themselves as new-comers to a well established group, 'regulars' and 'occasionals' perceive such short-term dancers as exceptional visitors, offering new interactive possibilities to be explored. All concerned have the impression of an ongoing collective of devotedly engaged persons, whereas in fact, for the most part, it is a continually recomposed assemblage of intermittently participating parties. In the case of 5 Rhythms and Movement Medicine, this illusion of stability derives in part from the presence of the instructor's 'team' in charge of cleaning and setting up the dance floor, welcoming the dancers, collecting entrance fees, and orienting newcomers. Data regarding three teams (numbering ten, five, and twelve individuals respectively) over a six-month period show that a majority of team members attend at least half of the sessions, two or three of them being present almost every time. Participants changing their clothes or waiting in the queue to pay before sessions, can see that team members know a great many dancers and have a long-standing familiarity with the group. They say attendees' names, give each other long hugs, and ask for news about people who are absent. Because they are among the most assiduous attendees who establish special relationships with a large number of participants, 'regulars', 'occasionals' and 'transients' alike, one may imagine that quite a number of dancers feel a stronger connection with team members than with the instructor. As a result, even if many of them do not always attend, their supposed presence, as evidenced by those who do, gives a sense of continuity to a series of successive sessions even if the group is a brand new assemblage every time.

Attendance, then, is characterized by a high turnover, but also by a distinctively diffuse, decentralized mode of participation. A core of regular participants does exist, but it is remarkably small. Moreover, those who make up this core are fairly inconstant. In the case of Biodanza, for example, they participate only 50 per cent or more of the time, and miss, on average, between one third and two fifths of their group's sessions. However, their participation is staggered in a mutually complementary fashion, each attending person filling in as it were for what is presumed to be the momentary absence of others. This stochastic, distributive principle applies not only to 'regulars' and 'occasionals', but to all attendees, the increasingly intermittent participation of a progressively expanding number of persons compensating for the periodic absences of more assiduous dancers. Thus, while it remains that some individuals participate more than others, as a general rule, the group persists as an identifiable entity less because some members participate most of the time, than because most participate some of the time. In other words, a dance group's viability as such is not founded on the existence of a strong, stable centre supplemented by a weak and largely superfluous periphery. Rather it relies on another, more complex, distributed dynamic in which most participants tend not to pursue a single activity to the exclusion of others, but to be successively or simultaneously involved in a plurality of loosely interconnected practices.

This distributed mode of participation can be seen as the expression, on the level of overall social form, of the ideological premise that has been shown to underlie much of the content of these dance practices, namely the idea that personal autonomy and collective solidarity go hand in hand. By partaking in a diversity of more or less related practices with others, participants explore and exhibit, in ways that are coherent with their personal histories and desires, both their capacities for individual freedom and expression *and* their propensities for constructive social interaction and group sentiment. This diffuse mode of participation is of course congruent with Gerlach and Hine's (1970) concept of a Segmented Polycentric Integrated Network (SPIN), a non-centralized reticulate social structure whose many, continuously emerging and evolving constituent groups are linked through cross-cutting connections. York (1995) has argued that this organizational model applies to New Age and contemporary Pagan movements (and on a higher level, as a SPIN of SPINS, to the contemporary 'holistic movement' as a whole), and the attendance patterns characteristic of dances of self-development clearly bear this out. However, it is important to note, as York also points out, that the concept of the SPIN pertains to 'change-oriented movements' in general, and was developed in connection with a study of US social movements of the 1960s and 1970s. From this point of view, in spite of the apolitical nature of the dance practices we have been looking at, there exists a definite formal affinity between these practices and those explicitly advocating participatory democracy, in which individual freedom and collective commitment are also posited as interdependent principles. In the following section we try to clarify, in the light of the preceding analyses, the relationship between dances of self-development and contemporary forms of political activism.

Dance as a Ritual Resource

New forms of political engagement have flourished over the last fifty years. Increasingly, organizational principles typical of more traditional political structures—hierarchy, impersonal allegiance, representation, male dominance, enduring membership—have given way to more direct, egalitarian and personalized patterns of activism. As a number of analysts have suggested, the restructuring of political activism since the 1970s is related to a progressive decentralization of the public sphere, but also to an increased emphasis placed on individual agency. For example, Ion (2001, 2012), in arguing against the widely held view that contemporary individualism has caused a decline of interest in political matters, reminds us, citing Singly (2003), that the abstract, 'anonymous' individuals of the Enlightenment endowed with statuses and roles have been increasingly replaced by reflexive, 'singular' individuals whose value is supposed to reside in their autonomy and distinctive personal qualities. Drawing on this idea and on his own extensive empirical work, he contends that this process of individuation at work in present-day Western society has brought about a more widespread degree of activism, notably through new forms of political engagement entailing highly mobile, informal, individual-based assemblies and networks. In social movement communities such as these, he suggests, personal autonomy and collective solidarity are deemed inseparable, such that 'nothing would be more mistaken than to oppose the individual and the collective' (2012: 73). Indeed, 'the collective …is less an aggregate than a site where individualities meet up, where, in the absence of pre-established roles, they come to find others who might resemble them, and to comfort their own ever-evolving identities'(2012: 56).

Dances of self-development and democratically inspired social movements are comparable in some respects, but not in others. They imply analogous, 'distributed' patterns of participation, for example, that attest to a common concern for making personal autonomy and collective commitment as compatible as possible. At the same time, in these dance practices, decision making, conflict resolution, and the recruitment of leadership teams are pointedly not organized along democratic lines, but remain the sole responsibility of the facilitator. Similarly, the ideological and performative precepts that underlie most social movements—individual freedom, diversity of opinion, openness to others, collective solidarity, etc.—are not unlike those enacted during dance sessions. However, the latter replace speech with music and bodily movement, and are organized around intense interpersonal encounters rather than shared political action. So how might we understand the relationship between radically democratic political activism on the one hand, and dances of self-development and other 'alternative' spiritual and/ or well-being practices on the other? In a functionalist nutshell, we see this relationship as potentially two-fold: while the former provides a support-ive context for the latter, the latter provides an essential resource for the former. On the one hand, radically democratic movements configure the encompassing social milieu in terms of issues and contrasts—oppression vs. liberty, socialization vs. creativity, exploitation vs. generosity, insensi-tivity vs. feeling, secrecy vs. openness, etc.—that contribute to the ongoing relevance and legitimacy of these dance (and other) practices. On the other hand, and it is the possibility of this second causal arc that is of special interest to us here, the distinctive sociality these practices put into effect can act as a widely accessible touchstone for the relational underpinnings that participatory democratic initiatives require: a sociability in which individual autonomy, heart-felt consideration of others and collective responsibility are expressively melded.

In her ground-breaking study of American social movements, Francesca Polletta insists that effective participatory democracy entails less a principle of strict equality than it does 'a more complex equality in which different skills, talents, and interests are seen as equally valuable' (2002: viii). Parity of this order, she observes, is found in a number of familiar relationships that have provided normative frameworks for the structuring of deliberative processes within social movements: family ties, religious fellowship, tute-lage, and especially friendship. By treating each other as friends, activists introduce 'not only broad injunctions against competition and manipulation but also micro-interactional rules about how to raise issues, frame disagree-ments, formulate (and even feel about) dissent' in ways that treat 'differ-ences in skills and preferences as sources of mutual learning rather than as obstacles to equality' (4). The 'participatory democratic dilemma', however, is that 'the very relationships generating trust and respect that democracy requires may also come with norms that undercut a democratic project' (221). For example, intrinsic qualities of friendship such as exclusivity, con-flict avoidance, and antipathy for rules pose challenges that many social movements have been unable to overcome. Polletta concludes that because formal procedures are not enough to ensure cooperative, egalitarian decision-making, it is necessary 'to develop new kinds of democratic relationships, ones that maximise the mutual respect, trust, and concern characteristic of formally nonpolitical relationships but avoid their weaknesses' (218). She mentions various attempts to do this (affinity groups, consciousness rais-ing groups, workshops, residential clusters, etc.) and outlines a number of guiding principles such initiatives might follow. Participants of successful social movements must behave in ways that are unlike conventional political interaction. At the same time, however, they must also behave in ways that are unlike what is expected of them in their everyday interactions at work, as family members and as friends. In light of this, Polletta assumes that innovative democratic patterns need to be created more or less from scratch, and warns against the difficulties raised by introducing such unfamiliar and therefore fragile relational forms.

Here, we venture to suggest, collective dance practices, and more generally, the entire SPIN of interrelated 'alternative' spiritual and well-being activities, may play an important role as sources of inspiration for the 'new kinds of democratic relationships' Polletta recommends. Self-development practices like collective dancing afford practitioners with memorable, highly reflexive, bodily experiences of mutual respect, trust, and concern in social settings in which individual autonomy and collective solidarity are made to systematically converge. Moreover, these settings are upheld by decentralised, distributed modes of participation formally similar to those characteristic of contemporary activism. As such, these practices would seem to be particularly well-suited to act as references for the political implementation of interactive forms that aim to 'maximize solidarity without denying differences' (224).

Normative relational frameworks other than friendship exist for the structuring of deliberative processes within social movements. In a recent review article on 'Participatory Democracy in the New Millennium' (2013), for example, Polletta herself identifies the influence, but also the possible deleterious, diluting effects of both online networks and the increasingly widespread, pragmatic recourse to decentralized, consensus-based decision-making in for-profit, non-profit, and governmental organizations. Here again is evidence of the aspirations of participatory democratic movements being subverted by features of the relational models they make use of. The *ritual* character of self-development practices like collective dancing, however, may be a hedge against this 'participatory democratic dilemma'. As argued elsewhere (Houseman, Mazzella di Bosco, and Thibault 2016, Houseman in press), 5 Rhythms, Movement Medicine, Biodanza and the like are crafted as rituals. Participants are enjoined to feel and act in ways that engender and/or express emotional and intentional dispositions that are held to have value in and of themselves: spontaneity, personal creativity and autonomy, respect and concern for others, solidarity towards the group, and so forth. However, these injunctions also lead participants to adopt the paradoxical posture of being purposefully spontaneous, distantly intimate, and collectively individualistic, such that, as we have seen, their exemplary experiences are perceived as clearly distinct from those of everyday interaction. They become imbued with a measure of self-referential authority and efficacy that allows them to be 'disembedded' from their immediate social context and brought to bear in circumstances beyond the dance sessions themselves. However, when these extra-ordinary ways of feeling and acting are mobilized beyond the dance floor, it is not as normative frameworks to be directly applied. Indeed, ritual experiences can rarely if ever act as realistic, viable models for routine interactions and relationships. Rather, they intervene as touchstone *revelations* or sources of inspiration, that is, as largely irrefutable yet difficult-to-define, 'privileged' (Bell 1992) yardsticks in the light of which routine interactions and relationships can be conventionally assessed (Houseman 2006).

It is important to stress that these 'revelations' are not about how participants should act, but about how they can be. Many social movement theorists, especially those concerned with emotions (e.g. Goodwin, Jasper and Polletta 2001), stress the importance of ritual, both as an authoritative basis for deliberative procedures, and as an expression of shared identity addressed at once outwards and to the actors themselves. This is surely true for social movements as it is for many other collective undertakings. However, the type of ritualization that occurs in dances of self-development and other 'alternative' spiritual and well-being practices is of a different order, one perhaps more adapted to the collective individualism that contemporary forms of participatory democracy seem to imply. Unlike more canonical ritual performances, these practices do not consist in undertaking mysterious yet 'archetypal' actions (Humphrey and Laidlaw 1994) that delineate special relationships, but in evincing enigmatic yet exemplary dispositions that distinguish special subjects (Houseman 2007, 2016). They do not consecrate the doing of what more authoritative others are supposed to have done, but the becoming of what more authoritative others are purported to have been. To the extent that these 'more authoritative others' are deemed to be aspects of the participants themselves (e.g. their 'inner child', 'spiritual side', 'potential for growth', etc.) such ritual practices afford them with the experience of becoming whom they feel they are meant to be. More concretely, these rituals do not define particular ways of being creative and spontaneous, of entertaining authentic, respectful relations with others, or of being committed to the group. Instead, they make manifest individual participants' capacity for finding their own personal ways of doing so. Dances of self-development, then, as part of a SPIN (of SPINs) of similarly ritualized practices, may be seen as a special, familiar and extensively developed resource for participatory democracy. They provide less regulatory models of behaviour in which personal freedom and collective solidarity are reconciled, than experienced individuals in whom this integration of opposites is supposed to have occurred.

References

Arendt, Hannah (1951), *The Origins of Totalitarianism*. London: Allen & Unwin.

Aupers, Stef, and Dick Houtman (2014), 'Beyond the spiritual supermarket: the social and public significance of new Age spirituality', in Steven J. Sutcliffe and Ingvild Saelid Gilhus, eds., *New Age Spirituality. Rethinking Religion*. London: Routledge. https://doi.org/10.1163/15700593-01501016.

Bell, Catherine (1992), *Ritual Theory, Ritual Practice*. New York: Oxford University Press.

Corrywright, Dominic (2003), *Theoretical and Empirical Investigations into New Age Spiritualities*. Oxford: Peter Lang.

Csikszentmihalyi, Mihaly (1990), *Flow: The Psychology of Optimal Experience*. New York: Harper and Row.

Fingerman, Karen L. (2009), 'Consequential Strangers and Periferal Partners: The Importance of Unimportant Relationships', *Journal of Family Theory and Review*, 1: 69–86. https://doi.org/10.1111/j.1756-2589.2009.00010.x.

Gerlach, Luther, and Virginia H. Hine (1970), *People, Power, Change: Movements of Social Transformation*. Indianapolis: Bobbs-Merrill.

Giddens, Anthony (1991), *Modernity and Self-Identity. Self and Society in the Late Modern Age*. Cambridge: Blackwell.

Goffman, Erving (1961), *Encounters. Two Studies in the Sociology of Interaction*. Indianapolis: Bobbs-Merril.

Goodwin, Jeff, Jasper M. James, and Francesca Polletta, eds. (2001), *Passionate Politics. Emotions and Social Movements*. Chicago: University of Chicago Press. https://doi.org/10.7208/chicago/9780226304007.001.0001.

Hamilton, M. B. (2000), 'An Analysis of the Festival for Body-Mind-Spirit, London', in Steven Sutcliffe and Marion Bowman, eds., *Beyond New Age: Exploring Alternative Spirituality*. Edinburgh: Edinburgh University Press, 188–200.

Heelas, Paul (1996), *The New Age Movement*. Cambridge: Blackwell.

Houseman, Michael (2006), 'Relationality', in Jens Kreinath, Joannes Snoek and Michael Stausberg, eds., *Theorizing Rituals. Issues, Topics, Approaches, Concepts*. Leiden: Brill, 413–428. https://doi.org/10.1111/j.1469-8676.2008.00052_12.x.

Houseman, Michael, (2007), 'Menstrual Slaps and First Blood Celebrations. Inference, Simulation and the Learning of Ritual', in David Berliner and Ramon Sarró, eds., *Learning Religion: Anthropological Approaches*. New York: Berghahn Books, 31–48.

Houseman, Michael (2016), 'Comment comprendre l'esthétique affectée des céré-
monies New Age et néopaïennes?', *Archives de Sciences Sociales des Religions,*
174: 213–237. https://doi.org/10.4000/assr.27807.

Houseman Michael, (in press), 'Becoming Autonomous Together: Distanced
Intimacy in Dances of Self-development', in Jone Salomonsen, Michael
Houseman, Sarah Pike, and Graham Harvey, eds., *Reassembling Democracy :
Ritual as Cultural Resource.* London: Bloomsbury Publishing.

Houseman, Michael, Marie Mazzella di Bosco and Emmanuel Thibault (2016),
'Renaître à soi-même. Pratiques de danses rituelles en Occident contemporain',
Terrain, 66: 62–85. https://doi.org/10.4000/terrain.15974.

Humphrey, Caroline, and James Laidlaw (1994), *The Archetypal Actions of Ritual. A
Theory of Ritual Illustrated by the Jain Rite of Worship.* Oxford: Clarendon Press.

Ion, Jacques, ed. (2001), *L'engagement au pluriel.* Saint Etienne: Presses universitaires de Saint Etienne. https://doi.org/10.7202/007901ar.

Ion, Jacques (2012), *S'engager dans une société d'individus.* Paris: Armand Colin.

Le Bart, Christian (2008), *L'individualisation.* Paris: Presses de la Fondation
Nationale de Sciences Politiques.

Lombardi, Denise (2016), *Parcours et pratiques dans le néo-chamanisme contemporain en France et en Italie.* Doctoral thesis, Ecole Pratique des Hautes Etudes,
Paris. https://doi.org/10.4000/ashp.860.

Luckmann, Thomas (1996), 'The Privatisation of Religion and Morality', in
Paul Heelas, Scott Lash, and Paul Morris, eds, *Detraditionalization: Critical
Reflections on Authority and Identity,* Cambridge: Blackwell Publishers, 72–86.

Marche, Guillaume (2012), 'Why Infrapolitics Matters', *Revue française d'études
américaines,* 131/3: 3–18. https://doi.org/10.3917/rfea.131.0003.

Marquis, Nicolas (2014), *Du bien-être au marché du malaise: La société du dével-
oppement personnel.* Paris: Presses Universitaires de France.
https://doi.org/10.3917/puf.marq.2014.01.

Miller, Daniel (1998), *A Theory of Shopping.* Cambridge: Polity Press.

Polletta, Francesca (2002), *Freedom is an Endless Meeting. Democracy in American
Social Movements.* Chicago: University of Chicago Press.
https://doi.org/10.7208/chicago/9780226924281.001.0001.

Polletta, Francesca (2013), 'Participatory Democracy in the New Millennium', *Contemporary Sociology,* 42/1: 40–50. https://doi.org/10.1177/0094306112468718b.

Prince, Ruth, and Davis Riches (2000), *The New Age in Glastonbury: The
Construction of Religious Movements.* New York: Berghahn Books.

Roof, Wade Clark (1999). *Spiritual Marketplace: Baby Boomers and the Remaking
of American Religion.* Princeton: Princeton University Press.
https://doi.org/10.1177/004057360205900131.

Roth, Gabrielle (1998), *Sweat Your Prayers: Movement as Spiritual Practice.* New
York: Archer Perigee.

Scott, James C. (1990), *Domination and the Arts of Resistance: Hidden Transcripts.*
New Haven: Yale University Press.

Singly, François de (2003), *Les uns avec les autres: Quand l'individualisme crée du lien*. Paris : Armand Colin.

Solier, Isabelle de (2013), *Food and the Self: Consumption, Production and Material Culture*. London: Bloomsbury.

Taylor, Charles (2007), *A Secular Age*. Cambridge, MA: Harvard University Press.

Teisenhoffer, Viola (2015), *Pratiques et expériences rituelles dans l'umbanda du Temple Guaracy de Paris (France)*. *Doctoral thesis, Université Paris-Nanterre*.

Van Hove, H. (1999), 'L'émergence d'un marché spirituel', *Social Compass*, 46/2: 161–172. https://doi.org/10.1177/003776899046002005.

Wood, Matthew (2007), *Possession, Power and the New Age: Ambiguities of Authority in Neoliberal Societies*. Aldershot: Ashgate. https://doi.org/10.4324/9781315601588.

York, Michael (1995), *The Emerging Network. A Sociology of the New Age and Neo-Pagan Movements*. Lanham, MD: Rowman & Littlefield.

About the Authors

Michael Houseman, anthropologist, is a directeur d'études (chair of African religions) at the Ecole Pratique des Hautes Etudes, PSL Research University (France). He has undertaken field research among the Beti of Southern Cameroon, in Benin, in French Guyana and in France. He has published extensively on kinship and social organization, and on initiation and ritual performance. His current areas of interest include ceremonial dance and emergent forms of ritual practice. His publications include *Naven or the Other Self. A Relational Approach to Ritual Action* (Brill, 1998, with C. Severi) and *Le rouge est le noir. Essais sur le ritual* (Presses Universitaires le Mirail, 2012).

Marie Mazzella di Bosco is a PhD candidate in anthropology in the Laboratoire d'ethnologie et de sociologie comparative (Paris Nanterre University). Her doctoral research focuses on mindful, free-form dances such as 5 Rhythms, Movement Medicine and Open Floor, and explores how these practices allow for a particular ritual production of participants' individual selves. For her master's degree she worked on Flamenco dance and the role of emotions in its cross-cultural transmission.

7. Trans-Indigenous Festivals: Democracy and Emplacement

Graham Harvey

Indigeneity and religion are both political categories entangled with the project of modernity and its approaches to nationhood and citizenship, and therefore to democracy. Indigenous peoples and religion as conceived[1] by the ideologues of modernity were (and often remain) largely excluded from political arenas except as negative exemplars. They are 'inclusive exclusions' (Agamben 1999: 217) that define and enforce membership of, and legitimate activity within, the constitution and conduct of nation states. However, the evolving performance of Indigeneity (often rooted in rituals and other customary practices) contests such exclusions even as it tests the boundaries of such inclusions.

This chapter discusses Indigenous[2] festivals and cultures because their deployment of rituals, etiquette, protocols and other practices is a key part of on-going Indigenous experiments in what democracy and citizenship might become. This is especially true of those ritually based activities rooted in customary or 'traditional' modes of peoplehood that are sensitive to the participation of other-than-human actors. The proffered entertainment that defines festivals and other performance cultures is, without ceasing to be infectiously and joyfully playful, braided into serious contests with and resistance to alienation, exclusion, and other facets of domination or colonization. Explicitly or implicitly, Indigenous festivals are laboratories in which participants experiment with ways of being human within larger-than-human polities. For some people, festivals are the context of a first intuition that Indigenous identities and/or lifeways can be positively valued. Some build on this by going on to claim citizenship of Indigenous nations (with or without rejecting nation-state identities) or to commit to greater degrees of involvement as Indigenous citizens. A range of other adjustments might be

---

1   'Conceived' because the project of modernity involves more than 'perceiving' and other seemingly more neutral acts.
2   The capitalization of "Indigenous" is discussed below.

made towards decolonisation, the affirmation of equal rights, and/or the taking of responsibility for (re-)establishing polities in which excluded humans and other-than-humans assemble together.

In the early sections of this chapter I present definitions of 'Indigeneity' and 'religion' which challenge their bracketing out or ghettoising away from 'modern' and 'rational' politics. This enables me to clarify a strategic definition of 'Indigenous religions' as having to do with belonging to (not 'in') places. In particular, I emphasise that in Indigenous contexts 'place' (and cognates like 'country') should be understood as larger-than-human communities rather than as mere scenery inhabited by marginalized human groups fixed within dominant nation states. Although many Indigenous people (and others) disavow the term 'religion', this has everything to do with the rhetoric and practices of nation states and their colonialism. As I will argue, religion was re-formed in early modernity (and then exported globally) to fit the requirements of citizenship within the new nation states. It was privatized and interiorized to curtail transnational affiliations. Relations with larger communities (including 'natural' and transcendent ones) and ritual practices were at the front line of the re-formation of early modern relations, affiliations and identities. Precisely those ritualized relations within larger-than-human communities are re-energized in Indigenous festivals. Therefore, Indigenous notions of peoplehood and community invite consideration of alternative understandings of sovereignty, citizenship and democracy. Revisiting 'religion' with an emphasis on the centrality of the rituals and etiquette of everyday relations with the larger-than-human world might not only enrich understanding of Indigenous performances and events, but also of democracy. This series of introductory orientations to Indigeneity and religion will be complemented by an overview of the relationship between contemporary trans-Indigenous performance cultures which involve both customary and novel forms and practices.

These programmatic considerations of scholarly definitions and perspectives form the entry point into reflections on the ways in which three selected Indigenous performance events push the boundaries of what 'democracy' and 'citizenship' might mean. In particular, they demand attention to relational and performative acts within larger-than-human polities of emplaced (but not bounded) multispecies communities. Politically speaking, the recognition of Indigenous rights at least requires understanding that a narrow focus on humans does not do justice to Indigenous ways of being and acting in, or moving through, the world. Once notice is paid to Indigenous relations with the larger-than-human community, the project of rethinking modernity, democracy, citizenship and religion may be further empowered. This chapter does not pursue the question of what precise political forms and forums particular Indigenous communities might restore or develop when their sovereign right to determine such matters makes this possible. However, it resonates with Marshall Sahlins' provocative argument that even the most egalitarian of such societies are segments of more 'inclusive cosmic polities, ordered and governed by divinities, ancestors, species-masters, and other such metapersons endowed with life-and-death powers over human populations' (Sahlins 2016: 91). In Indigenous festival performances, as in the re-assembling of Indigenous nationhood, relations with larger-than-human persons are often vital.

Defining Indigeneity Politically

I have been capitalizing the term 'Indigenous' to distinguish it from a wider, more general usage of lower-case 'indigenous'. The latter only notes that everyone and everything originated somewhere. Oranges, chickens and some humans are indigenous to Southeast Asia. Whether that is an interesting fact may depend on the context of its assertion. It does not seem significantly generative, unless perhaps we might learn something about cultures indigenous to that region and their relations to neighbouring, regional, and global alternatives. My capitalisation of 'Indigenous' here signals a more deliberate indicator of affiliation to communities in which the celebration of belonging to localities is simultaneously braided into transnational relations.

Precisely what defines the conditions under which a community should be recognized as Indigenous has been a contentious issue. Christopher Hartney and Daniel Tower's edited volume of essays *Religious Categories and the Construction of the Indigenous* (2016) provides many overlapping and sometimes vigorously competing approaches to the issue. Most helpfully, Hartney's concluding chapter proffers this important intervention:

> An indigenous tradition is one that continues to interrupt, problematise, and outright challenge the sovereignty claims of the modernist, post-colonial nation with its own claims of abiding sovereignty…. This [unique political place of indigenous communities] is the holding of claims to sovereignty that precede and may not necessarily be extinguished by the sovereignty of the 'modern' and 'rational' secular state….The 1933 Montevideo Convention of the Rights and Duties of States legally defines a state as, amongst other conditions, an entity that has the 'capacity to enter into relations with other states.' In light of this, the simplest way to identify an indigenous community is to demarcate a

community that is able to enter into relations, sympathies, and solidarities with other self-defined indigenous communities. (Hartney 2016: 221–2).

Comparison with the working definition employed by the United Nations Permanent Forum on Indigenous Issues (UNPFII) is instructive. Following a declaration that 'no formal universal definition of the term is necessary' the UNPFII's definition states that,

> Indigenous communities, peoples and nations are those which, having a historical continuity with pre-invasion and pre-colonial societies that developed on their territories, consider themselves distinct from other sectors of the societies now prevailing on those territories, or parts of them. They form at present non-dominant sectors of society and are determined to preserve, develop and transmit to future generations their ancestral territories, and their ethnic identity, as the basis of their continued existence as peoples, in accordance with their own cultural patterns, social institutions and legal system. (UNPFII 2004: 2)

The UNPFII's statement goes on to set out that the all-important 'historical continuity may consist of the continuation, for an extended period reaching into the present of one or more …. factors'. These include occupation of ancestral lands, common ancestry with the original occupants of those lands, culture (possibly including religion, dress, lifestyle etc.), language, residence and 'other relevant factors'. It is possible to read this as largely defining 'indigenous communities' as colonized minorities who are determined to maintain some form of ancestral identity while occupying land within the borders of dominant nation states. However, the UNPFII's recognition that such communities' determination to continue to exist is 'in accordance with their own cultural patterns, social institutions and legal system' points to something quite radical. This is the assertion of sovereignty rooted in what Hartney identifies as claims which 'precede and may not necessarily be extinguished' by the dominance of settler states (even if such states imagine and attempt such extinction).

The UNPFII document implies the importance of the 'capacity to enter into relations with other states' when it sets out who can be recognized as 'indigenous'. It notes that any individual may self-identify but that recognition by an Indigenous group is required before anyone can claim representative status. It seeks to preserve the 'sovereign right and power [of indigenous communities] to decide who belongs to them, without external interference'. Alongside the recognition of determination to act in accordance with 'their own cultural patterns, social institutions and legal system[s]', this preservation of sovereignty justifies the definition of Indigenous communities as 'nations' rather than merely as minority interest groups.

These affirmations of sovereignty preface reflections on the contribution made by Indigenous performance cultures and festival events to the preservation, development, transmission, and encouragement of Indigenous emplaced citizenship. Performances and festivals are not distractions even when they are thoroughly entertaining. Within processes of evolving customary rites and knowledges, such festivals provide contexts for establishing, maintaining, and enhancing relations between different Indigenous nations and communities. They also cultivate democratic sensibilities and cultures both by encouraging more active participation in such communities and by increasing an understanding that a 'community' is larger than, but inclusive of, the human polity. The inclusion of other-than-human persons is a necessary aspect of Indigenous community building and maintenance and, in turn, underpins Indigenous activism on behalf of the larger-than-human community in legal, political and other contexts. Such matters will be discussed further because they offer a dramatic challenge to dominant notions of sovereignty, nationhood, democracy and citizenship.

Defining Religion Politically

In recent decades there has been a 'turn' within the academic study of religion(s) towards researching and theorising religion as lived, vernacular, everyday, and material phenomena (e.g. Hall 1997; Orsi 1997, 2012; Primiano 1995, 2012; McGuire 2008; Vásquez 2011; Schielke and Debevec 2012; Harvey 2013; Plate 2015). This 'turn' attends to the *doing* of religion, or 'religioning' as Malory Nye (2000) proposed. It involves insistently developing ethnographic approaches to performative, material and gendered activities and processes. Nonetheless, the temptation to treat religion as a strange fusion of interiority and transcendence remains.

Despite widespread insistence that the 'World Religions Paradigm' is obsolete, school and university textbooks which privilege founders, creeds, scriptures, and the teachings of elite authorities as definitive of particular religions—and of the category 'religion'—remain far from exceptional. Religious people may well revere founders, defer to authorities, and cite texts. They might declare themselves to be 'believers' and they might believe in the existence of deities, angels, ancestors, ghosts, faeries, jinn, and so on. When this is the case there is no difficulty in making it the subject of discussion. However, the limiting of religion to such 'belief-ing' practices (Harvey 2013: 195)—let alone to the putative interiority of 'believing'— collapses what could be a significant arena of scholarly and public debate into the repetition of a small selection of available data. It is not enough to bring body and matter into a frame shaped by early modernity's formation of 'religion'. Rather, embodiment, materiality, and relationality radically contest the privatization and interiorization of religion. They also require us to attend to the inherently political nature of our approaches to religion(s).

The processes by which religion was (trans)formed deserve further examination. They are an integral and central aspect of the history of the establishment of modernity and its nation states, bureaucracies and modes of citizenship. To summarise William Cavanaugh's argument (1995, 2009): the construction of modern nation states necessitated the curtailment of allegiances which transgressed national borders and loyalties. Conflicts which devastated large areas of Europe have been misrepresented as 'Wars of Religion' rather than as wars to establish modern political practices. The Treaty of Westphalia (1648) did not so much end 'Wars of Religion' as legislate for modern state-making, inter-state relationships and citizenship. To a large degree, such events and processes have created an illusion that nation states were progressive whilst religions (among other transnational networks) were regressive. The political goal of limiting the allegiances of citizens solely to the princes and bureaucracies of specific (bordered) nation states was integral to the rationalization of the new order and demanded the contributory mechanism of the privatization and interiorization of religion. Thus, religion could only be allowed to survive as a practice of believing in matters marginal (at best) to modern politics and polities, as 'licensed insanities' (Bowker 1987) or 'licensed impracticalities' or mere hobbies (Harvey 2015: 191–2).

However, if as the title of one of Bruno Latour's works asserts, 'we have never been modern' (1993), this is partly because religion has continued to be important in both everyday contexts and in the form of publically affirmed transnational loyalties. As Robert Orsi argues, many people have not fully capitulated to the requirement to conduct only a 'modern liberal faith sanctioned by (and providing sanction for) law, political theory, epistemology and science' (2012: 146). Nonetheless, again following Chris Hartney, if scholars and others continue to 'exclude the state' and the political from our definitions, approaches and methods, we will find that our 'un-political definitions have immured us deeper and deeper into equally a political, a mythic, and a religious quest' and that we have become 'boundary maintainers for the faith system we know more commonly as "modernity"' (Hartney 2016:

224). In short, we need to resist William James' experiment of 'arbitrarily' taking religion to mean:

> *the feelings, acts, and experiences of individual men in their solitude, so far as they apprehend themselves to stand in relation to whatever they may consider the divine.* (James 1997 [1902]: 42; italics in original)

We need to understand that both religion and the study of religion are political activities.

David Chidester helpfully proposes that religion should be thought of as,

> an open set of resources and strategies for negotiating a human identity, which is poised between the more than human and the less than human, in the struggles to work out the terms and conditions for living in a human place oriented in sacred space and sacred time. (2012: ix)

This is also true of political institutions and processes. For example, parliaments and congresses (prime contexts for negotiating human identities and activities) have a sacral, elevated set-apartness, illustrated at times when flags and manifestos are paraded (Lynch 2012). The openness of religious and political resources and strategies is shaped (rather than limited) by their reference to what Jim Cox calls 'an overpowering authoritative tradition that is passed on from generation to generation' (2016: 39). In turn, as Cox (2016: 55–6) says of religion, these traditions are dynamic, adaptive, adoptive and persistent. Chidester goes further in presenting the 'wild, surprising creativity' of Indigenous religions (2012: ix)—'surprising' because they are conventionally portrayed as static and uniform. Instead, improvisational fluidity is definitive of 'tradition' as most Indigenous people (and many [other] religious people) use it. This will shortly be demonstrated by reference to Robert Jahnke's (2006) and Chadwick Allen's (2012) reflections on trans-customary and trans-Indigenous arts.

There are many proposals as to how to formulate a new definition of 'religion' and about what ingredients or characteristics may appropriately be drawn from specific religions for this purpose. This chapter will neither rehearse nor complete that work. However, interests in Indigenous cultural knowledges and practices, politics and protocols invite consideration of placing religious activities among the varied modes of 'interpersonal engagement of human and other-than-human persons' (Morrison 2000: 36; also see Harvey 2013). That is, it encourages the experiment of locating religion not among peculiar hobbies but among those everyday and political negotiations which seek better ways to live alongside other persons (of whatever species). If religion is re-placed among the legitimate acts and allegiances of citizens, it invites the transgressing of early modernity's boundary constructions. Not only might religious practices express and shape transnational relations but they might also anticipate Giorgio Agamben's 'coming politics' in which the 'inclusive exclusion' (i.e. the definitive marginalization) of animals and other 'natural life' will be reintegrated (1999: 217; also see 1995: 3).

The following sections consider what 'Indigenous religions' means and then illustrate trans-Indigenous performance events in which a larger-than-human polity is included. They argue that Indigenous religious and cultural practices and knowledges emphasise human relations and communal belonging with and among (other) animals and other citizens of the larger-than-human world.

Placing Indigenous Religions

The strategic aim of increasing attention to Indigenous religions (Harvey 2017) could be well served by attending to emphases on land, place, and/or emplacement. This is not to acquiesce to the notion that there are 'universal religions' to contrast with 'local religions', or that only some religions have a universal message or global relevance. Indeed, it invites attention to relationships between all persons and places (persons are, after all, bodies moving through places) and to those between particular religious practices and the lands or locations in which they are performed. There is a specificity about graves, pilgrimage venues, sites of revelation, fields where crops are blessed, and the many religious buildings at the heart of communities. In contrast, even supposedly universal religions diversify in encounters with local conditions and experiences, i.e. Christianity, Islam, and Buddhism are not the same everywhere. What makes Indigenous traditions distinctive is not their constriction within a fixed temporality or geography but their deliberate, explicit and programmatic emphasis on place as community. These are not, and never have been, securely bounded or bordered places from which people and practices cannot move. They are always places from which people go out and go in. They are homelands, not boxes or prisons.

The Yidindji (Aboriginal) ex-journalist Murrumu Walubara Yidindji defines Indigeneity when he says, '*Superficies solo credit*—what is attached to the land belongs to the land' (Daley 2014). He refers to the attachment of humans, of multispeces communities, and of buildings and infrastructure located on ancestral lands. To be clear, he is making a claim to ownership (rights and responsibilities) of all that exists within his people's country. This contrasts with the unsettled and unsettling expansionism of those who imagine themselves, their religions, and all their (cultural and material) constructions to belong everywhere without belonging to anywhere. Daley's localising trajectory (stressing a 'belonging to' particular originating places) is a key aspect of what Paul Johnson (2002) identifies as 'indigenizing' (in contrast with 'universalising'): the practice of relating everything (customary or novel) to local, traditional or customary behaviours, values and worldviews.

Within the larger frame of religion as the 'interpersonal engagement of human and other-than-human persons', to borrow Morrison's (2000: 36) phrase, there are specific practices and activities that compose and vitalise Indigenous communal relations. Deborah Bird Rose (1998, 2004) restores the meaning 'clan' to the originally (Native American) Anishinaabe term 'totem'. This enables her to speak freshly about 'totemism' as relations between species who, finding themselves co-located, are expected to commit themselves to each other's 'flourishing in the world'. If this form of totemism conveys a sense of Indigenous communities and polities, it is also braided with the expectation that ritual practices will contribute significantly to cross-species assembly, communication, socialization, cooperation or negotiation. Religion, in this light, is reclaimed as a political activity for a larger-than-human world.

In summary, 'Indigenous religions' refers to enacted relationships between humans and the emplaced larger-than-human community into which they are born. It involves learning and improvising on transmitted customary ways of interacting respectfully with others (human or other-than-human), seeking to understand and enhance their ways of being in lands or locations. Ritual, ceremony, or etiquette may be framed as key modes of relating between persons (human or otherwise). These ways of interacting underlie many of the performances offered in festivals and other cultural events to Indigenous and wider communities and audiences by Indigenous actors, musicians, artists, and others. Therefore, the following section is an orientation to contemporary trans-Indigenous performance cultures.

Trans-Indigenous Performance Cultures

A valuable distinction is made by Robert Jahnke in relation to Indigenous visual art, and elaborated on by Chadwick Allen in relation to Indigenous literature. In Allen's summary,

Māori artist and art scholar Robert Jahnke has developed a conceptual model for contemporary Māori visual art that imagines a continuum running between the pole 'customary' (art created by Māori that maintains 'a visual correspondence with historical models') and its opposite pole, 'non-customary' (art created by Māori in which 'visual correspondence and empathy with historical models [is] absent'). Much of contemporary Māori art is produced in the vast middle space between these poles, Jahnke argues, and it is neither 'hybrid' nor caught 'between' but 'trans-customary': art that establishes not a strict correspondence with customary forms but rather a 'visual empathy with customary practice' through the use of 'pattern, form, medium and technique'. (Allen 2012: 153, citing Jahnke 2006: 48–50)

Allen emphasises that Jahnke's key distinction is between strict correspondence with customary *forms* (i.e. precise replications of previous cultural products) and empathy with customary *practice* (i.e. adaptive improvisations or riffs on ways of working and living).

The 'vast middle space' of trans-customary practice becomes the domain of the 'trans-Indigenous' in Allen's own extensive discussion of 'global native literary studies'. The trans-Indigenous is the juxtaposition and assembling together of interacting communities and cultures, speakers and listeners in a richly storied world, and of actors, entertainers, educators, and their audiences and respondents. Most of the performing and visual arts at Indigenous festivals are in that trans-Indigenous trans-customary mode. Patterns, forms, media, and techniques draw on inherited customary practices to produce improvisations that are recognisably Indigenous and contemporary. The juxtaposing of the inherited with the contemporary makes work that is necessary and generative.

One virtue of this intervention by Jahnke and Allen is that it sets aside unhelpful polemics about 'authenticity' which tend to privilege imagined pre-contact practices over contemporary 'pan-Indian' or 'pan-Indigenous' 'hybridity' or 'syncretism'. It contests over-rehearsed notions of the fixity or boundedness of tradition and of Indigenous cultures and lifeways. Instead, It reinforces emphases on Indigenous rights to self-representation and communal self-determination (aspects of the sovereignty of nationhood and/or peoplehood). As these are enshrined in the United Nations Declarations on the Rights of Indigenous Peoples (cited above) I can move on to illustrate ways in which Indigenous performance events relate to processes of democratisation. A Mi'kmaq powwow, a Sámi organized festival and a biennial cultural festival in London provide case-studies in which a tapestry of issues are woven together.

Powwows and Eagles

In 1995 I attended the first annual powwow hosted by the Miawpukek First Nation at the Conne River Reserve, Newfoundland, Canada. The powwow took place at the edge of this small Mi'kmaq community where the Conne River enters the Bay d'Espoir. All the powwows since 1995 have been billed as 'traditional' events, meaning that they are not competitive. Drummers and dancers come from the community, from other Mi'kmaq communities in Newfoundland and Canada's mainland, and from other First Nations and Native American communities further away. They participate to express and celebrate Indigenous identities and to evolve protocols and practices relevant to contemporary Indigenous lives. They certainly enjoy themselves and there is a degree of competition for recognition by drum groups and the different styles of dancer. Increasing numbers of Euro-Canadian and other 'white' tourists join local people and other Mi'kmaq participants in the appreciative audiences for these three-day events.

Local crafts makers and artists display their work. There are food stands offering traditional foods and powwow favourites such as fry-bread. There is an evening feast offered free to all participants but structured by the pervasive First Nations protocol by which elders are invited to be served first. Alongside the socialising and entertainment, these powwows contest (implicitly for the most part) the denigration of Indigeneity by some elements in the dominant (European origin) settler community. The drum and dance styles are predominantly those inherited from the Plains and Prairie cultures of the centre of North America, as these performance styles evolved in the late nineteenth to mid-twentieth centuries. Some localization of clothing and dance styles is evident as people present more Maritime / Atlantic seaboard styles of beadwork and other adornment and action. In short, these powwows are emblematic of 'trans-Indigenous' practices.

Miawpukek's powwows are a deliberate aspect of an Indigenization process, initiated by local people resisting their marginalization and impoverishment by the province and the state, and creatively restoring their own sovereign self-determination. Cultural practices and language re-acquisition work alongside a host of political, social, cultural, educational, and employment efforts to establish a more resilient and self-assured community. Not all members of the community embrace the specific ways in which revitalization is being pursued, but none wish for a return to the days of more assertive colonial domination. In this diverse context, one moment in the 1995 powwow illustrates the transformative potential of trans-Indigenous performance events for individuals and communities. At the end of that first powwow, an eagle flew a perfect circle over and around the drum group playing the last honour song as elders and veterans danced the last dance. I was not alone in expressing surprised pleasure. Locals too, hardly unfamiliar with eagles, stopped and exclaimed '*kitpu!*' or 'eagle!'. Afterwards several people told me, without my asking, that the eagle was affirming his or her pleasure at the efforts of the local human community to return to the traditional ways which eagles, bears and others had patiently maintained. A couple of younger people told me that the powwow and the eagle's flight made them proud for the first time about their Native or Indigenous heritage and identity. For those who had led the development of the powwow, the eagle's flight and these human responses to it, signalled success and they were encouraged to organize further powwows.

Riddu Riđđu, Mountains and Salmon

My second example focuses on the Riddu Riđđu festival hosted in Olmmáivággi (Manndalen in Norwegian) in the arctic municipality of Kåfjord in July each year since 1991. The festival's name means 'small storm at the coast'. Support from the Reassembling Democracy: Ritual as Cultural Resource (REDO) project[3] enabled me to attend the festival four times between 2011 and 2015 and to establish friendships so that I can continue discussing developments.

Riddu Riđđu was initiated in the wake of the Sámi cultural revival— or perhaps the revival of pride in being Sámi which preceded that cultural revival. Riddu Riđđu's website is updated each year, but always includes a summary of the history of the festival. The current 'history' page (Riddu 2020) is particularly useful in setting out the festival's evolution from youthful conversations at a barbeque in 1991 to an international cultural event of considerable significance. Riddu Riđđu has grown from being a storm of controversy about what it means to be Sámi, how to express sovereignty, and, for some, how to develop the resources of traditional culture, to being a storm of cultural creativity. It now attracts performers and artists from many Indigenous nations globally, alongside Sámi musicians and actors (presenting diverse genres). For example, it has include Māori bands, Mayan theatre groups, Mongolian throat-singers, Andean rappers, Khoi jazz poets, Cree

3   I am also grateful to Marianne Henriksen for skilful introductions to much of importance at the festival and in Sápmi—as well as for translations and help in getting to and from Kåfjord.

film directors, and many others. The majority of festival-goers are probably Sámi from the nearby locality and from across Sápmi (i.e. the homelands of the various Sámi populations now within Norway, Sweden, Finland and Russia). However, busses from regional airports (Tromsø and Alta) enable significant attendance by broader national and international audiences, many of them Indigenous. For all the excitement of festivity and spectacle, Riddu Riđđu has never lost its vision of encouraging and enhancing participation in Sámi and other Indigenous communities and cultures, and of contesting Indigenous marginalization in cultural, political, economic and other arenas. The festival's demonstration of Indigenous creativity and global connectedness promotes self-determination and self-representation as vital aspects of Indigenous sovereignty. In these and other ways (further discussed below), Riddu Riđđu expands the possibilities for understanding democracy.

The main festival site is in a bend in a river flowing from the mountains to the nearby fjord. A permanent cultural centre (the Center for Northern People) houses the organisers' offices, a library, gallery and seminar rooms, a performance space, showers, and other facilities useful both for the festival and for local people outside of festival times. The site has a main stage area and nearby spaces that become a market place for indigenous goods, and the location of bars for alcoholic and soft drinks. Several food outlets are set up during the festival. A permanent cedar-log longhouse (constructed in a style traditional among the Nisga'a First Nation from British Columbia, Canada) is the most prominent construction in an otherwise temporary cultural village in which an earth lodge, lavvus (Sámi tents), tipis, small marquees, and other structures are used during the festival for various events and displays. The festival has two main camping areas, a 'party field' near the main site and one further away up a hill for families and those desiring a quieter environment (during the continuous daylight of the arctic summer the sleep patterns of festival-goers do not always coincide). There is a youth camp in which local youths meet each year with others invited from another Indigenous nation (e.g. Ainu or Evenki) to learn and party together. The festival also has a parallel children's programme, including both educational and entertainment events. In addition to main stage concerts, there are theatrical performances, talks and seminars, art exhibitions, book launches and other literary events, and film shows in the cultural centre or in the cedar log-house.

The trans-customary and trans-Indigenous nature of Riddu Riđđu's performance culture is most evident on the main stage. A Tuvan zither (a *yat kha*) might be played to accompany not only the Tuvan *kanzat kargyraa* throat-singing style, but also Indigenized reggae, rock, or country genres.

First Nation Canadian and Māori bands invite Sámi colleagues to meld yoik chants into their performances. The 'vast middle space' of Jahnke and Allen's trans-Indigenous practice and production is strongly evoked by frequent references to the authority of Nils-Aslak Valkepää, the late poet-laureate of Sápmi, whose revitalization of yoik as a contemporary art form with historical inspiration is widely celebrated. Similarly, in her several appearances at Riddu Riđđu festivals, Moana (lead singer of Moana and the Tribe) has opened her band's set by calling 'From our mountains to your mountains, from our rivers to your rivers'. This translates an element of traditional Māori greetings for varied purposes, including locating performers and audiences in relation to places of origin, honouring the local (Indigenous) land, placing visitors and hosts in relation to Indigenous traditional knowledges and protocols, and acknowledging that mountains and rivers welcome guests and involve humans in relationships. Altogether, these different elements of Moana's greeting reinforce central and definitive aspects of Indigeneity and propel the indigenizing project.

The vital importance of knowing homelands (one meaning of 'ecology') was most clearly expressed to me in a conversation in 2014. The river that flows around three sides of the Riddu Riđđu festival site had come close to flooding the area. Global climate change had led to the ice on the mountains melting faster and in greater quantities than usual. As I watched the river overflowing rocks on which ravens often sit, a local man told me, 'This isn't good for us, but it's a disaster for the trout and even more so the salmon'. He explained that the fish were currently waiting to swim up the river to spawn. He said that they too have their homelands, their Indigeneity. The flow and near ice-cold temperature of the water prevented them. The man asserted that the trout might just find another river. But, he said, the salmon would only return to the river of their birth. If the river flow kept them away, there would be no more salmon in this river. I might have misremembered whether it was trout and salmon that are most particular about their rivers. Equally, the man might have been misinformed. My point in summarising the conversation is that this man appeared to be repeating what other local people were concerned about. The threat to fish has clear dangers to coastal Sámi livelihoods—and perhaps to aspects of the cultural renaissance Riddu Riđđu is encouraging. However, it was absolutely clear that concern for the well-being, lifeways and cultural customs of the fish and other river beings was the major issue for this man and others. No yoik was offered, only deep concern and a sense of regret that human greed had caused this problem.

The Origins Festival, Embassies and Ancestors

My third example of a trans-Indigenous performance event is the biennial Origins Festival of First Nations, hosted in London, UK. The event has been organized by Border Crossings since 2007 and brings Indigenous 'musicians, theatre-makers, visual artists, film-makers and cooks, to exhibit and explain, to perform and inform, to debate and celebrate' (Border Crossings 2017). Venues across London host diverse events including displays and dances in the British Museum, comedy and films at Rich Mix, ritual/theatre/ spectacle in a West End park, and art in galleries. Some of the participants visit schools to provide special intercultural educational opportunities for various age groups. The festival audiences are predominantly Londoners or otherwise British. However, there are events in which performers and other contributors to the festival meet together and enrich their understandings of the each other's cultural and artistic traditions. Much of what takes place is intended to be experienced by audiences as entertainment. Nonetheless, the primary goal of the festival is to highlight Indigenous perspectives on contemporary issues—including 'the environment, globalization, truth and reconciliation, and healing'—and to provide a forum in which audiences and opinion-formers can engage directly with Indigenous representatives.

Democracy is enhanced when people of diverse backgrounds and perspectives are able to engage in dialogue and improve their comprehension of others. The fact that some of the nation-states from which Indigenous people travel to London fund participation might also be celebrated as exemplifying increased recognition and inclusion of such groups and cultures by dominant political powers. The opening ceremonies are often attended by representatives from relevant embassies (e.g. of Australia, Canada, and Mexico). This is not to suggest that there is no friction—indeed, while performers pay respect to embassy / nation state officials, they often speak of *themselves* as ambassadors, diplomats, or other kinds of representative of their Indigenous nations. They can present their presence and performance in the metropolis of a previously (and still) imperial nation as a contest with colonialism or as a 'talking back' to power.

Like Miawpukek's powwows and the Riddu Riđđu festival, the Origins Festival provides many opportunities for raising the issue of Indigenous sovereignty and of the resilience of customary or traditional political and religious practices. In previous sections I have emphasized that Indigenous communities include animals, birds, fish, mountains and rivers. Similar relations may be spoken about by participants in the Origins Festival. In this section I draw attention to the inclusion of ancestors—or 'those who have died'[4]—within polities and communities as understood within many Indigenous cultures.

Indigenous engagements with such persons offer a powerful lens through which to re-examine democratic processes precisely because 'the dead' are routinely excluded from consideration as members of modern communities. The process by which this exclusion became routine and unremarkable requires a brief summary in order to highlight the contrasting practices of Indigeneity. The medieval European constitution of society involved a 'communion of saints' in which the living performed actions to aid their deceased relatives to access heaven and those 'saints' and 'souls' interceded with their deity on behalf of the living. One element of the Protestant assertion of 'salvation by faith alone' was the dismantling of that relational network. The forceful rejection and sometimes violent eradication of large swathes of ceremonial and material culture shaped early modern approaches to kinship, community and emplacement. These transformative processes were integral to the creation of modern polities and, therefore, to colonial challenges to Indigenous constructions of communities.

As Indigenous performers 'speak back' to empire in the Origins Festival, so too do the ancestors. Within the central precinct of the British Museum in 2015, the Zugubal Dancers (from Zenadth Kes, Torres Straits Islands) performed masked dances. A few years previously, when he saw masks which had been collected and given to the museum in the nineteenth century, Alick Tipoti, the Zugubal Dancers' director, promised those masks that he would bring a group to dance for them. The group danced privately for the ancestor masks and then for an appreciative audience during the Origins Festival. Tipoti explained to the audience that the group would follow customary etiquette and not smile while wearing masks (even when posing for photographs) because not only were the masks 'ancestral' but by wearing them, the dancers became the ancestors. For a while, the British Museum became a ritual space for renewing good relations with ancestors and for reinforcing better relations with potential allies in the continuing struggle for inclusion and/or sovereignty.

The Origins Festival provides further examples of active engagement with ancestors. Many acts begin with invocations and expressions of respect to them, and sometimes they are invited to address audiences through performers. Complex relations between communities of diverse ancestries— and different understandings of the term 'ancestor'—are assembled during

---

4   A phrase suggestive of the notion that death is a transformative moment in lives and relations.

the festival. Rituals provide templates from which improvisations allow inter-cultural exchanges. At the heart of even the most entertaining of festive acts there is a challenge to the project of modernity and its separation of (living) humans from all other possible beings. The nature of communities is questioned. Alternatives (to modernist) understandings and practices are proffered. Invitations to gain knowledge of performers' cultures initiate processes of inclusion in which Indigenous peoples are seen as contributors to various national, regional and global cultural exchanges. Audiences are invited to set aside romantic and colonial perspectives and to reflect on how things might be different. They are also challenged, explicitly or implicitly, to consider the legacy of European historical, cultural, and religious processes, and especially to re-imagine communities that embrace rather than exclude Indigenous peoples, ancestors, and the larger-than-human world.

Conclusion: Leaving the Citizen Ship for Ancestral Land

In his interview with Paul Daley (2014), Murrumu Walubara Yidindji talks about 'jumping off the citizen ship, leaving Australia' to return to being a 'tribal man' living on his ancestral land. The resonance of the 'ship' pun with colonial invasion and prison ships is not incidental to the conversation about belonging and possession. What is more vital and compelling is the sense that for this man—and his colleagues involved in re-affirming the sovereignty of the Yidindji nation—the primary focus is the return to landed-ness and emplaced belonging within larger-than-human communities.

The short evocations of Miawpukek's powwows, of Riddu Riđđu and of the Origins Festival similarly evoke the centrality of place as multi-species community. The Indigenous nations which many Indigenous peoples are evolving are trans-customary, like their artistic, literary and performance cultures. They draw on the resources and strategies of Indigenous interpersonal and communal relations, of historical and inherited authority patterns and protocols, of knowledges of the co-dwelling of multiple species that make up local and regional communities. These become, experimentally and with negotiation, the foundations for new ways of assembling and organising Indigenous nations and their relations with other sovereign peoples (whether these be settler nation states, other Indigenous nations or ex-Imperial powers). They invite a renegotiation of the concepts and practices resulting from early-modernity's state-making, inter-state relationships and models for citizenship.

At Indigenous performance events and festivals, people are encouraged (implicitly or explicitly, subtly or forcefully) to participate more fully in Indigenizing processes. For some, it is enough that more people dance or chant in ways informed by customary practices and modes. For some, it is enough that more people self-identify with local, regional, and global political processes which may increase Indigenous sovereignty. These and other results of Indigenous gatherings have to do with self-expression and self-determination and, as such, are already increases in democratic participation. The recovery of an acted-upon understanding that 'community', 'place', and 'kin' are terms for relationships that embrace more-than-human polities involves further steps deeper into an Indigenous and Indigenizing world. Seeing an eagle's flight as meaningful and communicative, seeing the plight of salmon as having more-than-economic or subsistence relevance, and seeing ancestral masks honoured again, all braid interests in land-rights, sovereignty, and international relations with ecology and relational ontologies. These feed back into celebrating the value of protocols and ceremonies of world-making on which Indigenous artistic performances and practices are commonly established.

As if all this was not enough, the mere fact of citizens from different Indigenous nations gathering together (whether as performers or audiences) already contributes to the establishing, maintaining and enhancing of relations between different Indigenous communities which justifies the assertion of nationhood. When recognized representatives of Indigenous nations engage together with each other, with visiting politicians from dominant settler states, or from international bodies like the UN, the conditions are ripe for the recognition of the 'capacity to enter into relations with other states' that defines statehood (Hartney 2016: 221–2). Finally, the religious underpinnings of Indigenous performance, especially those rooted in ritual, reinforce the argument that religion must be understood as a way of doing politics, i.e. of the structuring of inter-personal (larger-than-human) relationships which seek to increase democracy.

References

Agamben, Giorgio (1995), *Homo Sacer: Sovereign Power and Bare Life*. Stanford: Stanford University Press. https://doi.org/10.1017/s0034670500041851.

Agamben, Giorgio (1999), *Potentialities: Collected Essays in Philosophy.* Stanford: Stanford University Press.

Allen, Chadwick (2012), *Trans-Indigenous: Methodologies for Global Native Literary Studies*. Minneapolis: University of Minnesota Press. https://doi.org/10.5749/minnesota/9780816678181.001.0001.

Border Crossings (2017), 'Origins', http://originsproject.or.uk/origins.

Bowker, John (1987), *Licensed Insanities. Religions and Belief in God in the Contemporary World*. London, Darton, Longman and Todd. https://doi.org/10.1017/s003693060004000x.

Cavanaugh, William T. (1995), 'A Fire Strong Enough to Consume the House: "The Wars of Religion" and the Rise of the State', *Modern Theology*, 11/4: 397–420. https://doi.org/10.1111/j.1468-0025.1995.tb00073.x.

Cavanaugh, William T. (2009), *The Myth of Religious Violence: Secular Ideology and the Roots of Modern Conflict*. Oxford: Oxford University Press. https://doi.org/10.1093/acprof:oso/9780195385045.001.0001.

Chidester, David (2012), *Wild Religion: Tracking the Sacred in South Africa*. Berkeley: University of California Press. https://doi.org/10.1525/california/9780520273078.001.0001.

Cox, James (2016), 'Kinship and Location: In Defence of a Narrow Definition of Indigenous Religon', in Christopher Hartney and Daniel J. Tower, eds., *Religious Categories and the Construction of the Indigenous*. Leiden: Brill. 38–57. https://doi.org/10.1163/9789004328983_004.

Daley, Paul (2014), 'The Man Who Renounced Australia.' *The Guardian*. http://www.theguardian.com/world/postcolonial/2014/aug/26/-sp-the-man-who-renounced-australia, accessed 24 August 2017.

Hall, David D., ed. (1997), *Lived Religion in America: Toward a History of Practice*. Princeton, NJ: Princeton University Press.

Hartney, Christopher (2016), 'Indigenous or Non-Indigenous: Who Benefits from Narrow Definitions of Religion?', in Christopher Hartney and Daniel J. Tower, eds., *Religious Categories and the Construction of the Indigenous*. Leiden: Brill, 203–227. https://doi.org/10.1163/9789004328983_011.

Hartney, Christopher, and Daniel J. Tower, eds. (2016), *Religious Categories and the Construction of the Indigenous*. Leiden: Brill. https://doi.org/10.1163/9789004328983.

Harvey, Graham (2013), *Food, Sex and Strangers: Understanding Religion as Everyday Life*. New York: Routledge. https://doi.org/10.4324/9781315729572.

Harvey, Graham (2015), 'Food, Sex and Spirituality', in Curtis D. Coats and Monica M. Emerich, eds., *Practical Spiritualities in a Media Age*. London: Bloomsbury, 189–204.

Harvey, Graham (2017), 'Performing Indigeneity and Performing Guesthood', in Christopher Hartney and Daniel J. Tower, eds., *Religious Categories and the Construction of the Indigenous*. Leiden: Brill, 74–91. https://doi.org/10.1163/9789004328983_006.

Jahnke, Robert (2006), 'Māori Art towards the Millennium', in Malcolm Mulholland, ed., *State of the Māori Nation: Twenty-first Century Issues in Aotearoa*. Auckland: Reed, 41–51. https://doi.org/10.1177/003231870605800107.

James, William (1997) [1902], *The Varieties of Religious Experience: A Study in Human Nature*. New York: Simon & Schuster.

Johnson, Paul C. (2002), 'Migrating Bodies, Circulating Signs: Brazilian Candomblé, the Garifuna of the Caribbean, and the Category of Indigenous Religions', *History of Religions*, 41/4: 301–327. https://doi.org/10.1086/463690.

Latour, Bruno (1993), *We Have Never Been Modern*. New York: Harvester Wheatsheaf.

Lynch, Gordon (2012), *On the Sacred*. Durham: Acumen.

McGuire, Meredith B. (2008), *Lived Religion: Faith and Practice in Everyday Life*. Oxford: Oxford University Press.

Morrison, Kenneth (2000), 'The Cosmos as Intersubjective: Native American and Other-Than-Human Persons', in Graham Harvey, ed., *Indigenous Religions: A Companion*. London: Cassell, 23–36.

Nye, Malory (2000), 'Religion, Post-Religionism and Religioning: Religious Studies and Contemporary Cultural Debates', *Method and Theory in the Study of Religion*, 12/4: 447–476. https://doi.org/10.1163/157006800X00300.

Orsi, Robert A. (1997), 'Everyday Miracles: The Study of Lived Religion', in David D. Hall, ed., *Lived Religion in America: Toward a History of Practice*. Princeton, NJ: Princeton University Press, 3–21. https://doi.org/10.2307/3169898.

Orsi, Robert A. (2012), 'Afterword: Everyday Religion and the Contemporary World', in Samuli Schielke and Liza Debevec, eds., *Ordinary Lives and Grand Schemes: An Anthropology of Everyday Religion*. New York: Berghahn Books, 146–161. https://doi.org/10.1111/1467-9655.12242.

Plate, Brent S. (2015), *Key Terms in Material Religion*. London: Bloomsbury.

Primiano, Leonard N. (1995), 'Vernacular Religion and the Search for Method in Religious Folklife', *Western Folklore*, 54/1: 37–56. https://doi.org/10.2307/1499910.

Primiano, Leonard N. (2012), 'Manifestations of the Religious Vernacular: Ambiguity, Power, and Creativity', in Ülo Valk and Marion Bowman, eds., *Vernacular Religion in Everyday Life: Expressions of Belief*. London, Equinox, 382–394. https://doi.org/10.3986/sms.v18i0.2841.

Riddu Riđđu (2017), https://riddu.no/en/history-riddu-riddu, accessed 13 May 2020, accessed 25 July 2017.

Rose, Debbie B. (1998), 'Totemism, Regions, and Co-management in Aboriginal Australia'. Paper presented at Crossing Boundaries, International Association for the Study of Common Property 7th Annual Conference, Vancouver, June 10–14, http://dlc.dlib.indiana.edu/dlc/bitstream/handle/10535/1187/rose.pdf, accessed 31 August 2017.

Rose, Debbie B. (2004), *Reports from a Wild Country: Ethics for Decolonisation*. Sydney: University of New South Wales Press.

Sahlins, Marshall (2016), 'The Original Political Society', *HAU: Journal of Ethnographic Theory*, 7/2: 91–128. https://doi.org/10.14318/hau7.2.014.

Schielke, Samuli, and Liza Debevec, eds. (2012), *Ordinary Lives and Grand Schemes: An Anthropology of Everyday Religion*. New York: Berghahn Books.

Vásquez, Manuel A. (2011), *More than Belief: A Materialist Theory of Religion*. Oxford: Oxford University Press. https://doi.org/10.1111/j.1748-0922.2012.01618_9.x.

UNPFII (2004), 'The Concept of Indigenous Peoples', www.un.org/esa/socdev/unpfii/documents/workshop_data_background.doc, accessed 31 August 2017.

About the Author

Graham Harvey is professor of religious studies at The Open University, UK. His research and teaching largely concern the rituals and protocols through which various Indigenous people and Pagans engage with the larger-than-human world. His publications include *Food, Sex and Strangers: Understanding Religion as Everyday Life* (2013), *The Handbook of Contemporary Animism* (2013) and *Animism: Respecting the Living World* (2nd edition 2017). He is co-editor of the Routledge monograph series 'Vitality of Indigenous Religions'.

Index

with larger-than-human persons 141;
with places 67
relationships 58, 73, 75, 133, 135,
146–147, 156
between dances and political activism
131, 133; between host and guest
102; between migrants 102; between
religions 109; between ritual and
democracy 2, 7; networks 5, 68
release (of energies) 31, 38–40, 42
religio-cultural
identity 70; memory 73; power 67;
relations 74
religion 1, 18, 69, 98, 111, 139, 142, 144,
146
Abrahamic religions (Judaism,
Christianity, Islam) 110; beliefs 144;
conflict 5, 144; conversion 101;
definition 74, 143, 145; evolution
of 32; identities (religio-cultural)
70; Indigenous 139–40, 145–147;
memory (religio-cultural) 72; migrants
101; power (religio-cultural) 67;
privatization of 144; relations (religio-
cultural) 74; relationship among 109;
research methods 7; theory of 36;
World Religions 143
religious process 155
conflict 6; narratives 103; tradition—
politicization 3
renaissance (cultural, Riddu Riđđu) 152
repertoires
cultural 1; performative 3, 11, 16,
23–25, 106
Report
Democracy Watch 20; Gezi 13, 20;
KONDA 20
representations 31, 36, 38–40, 43, 44, 49,
57–58, 79, 108, 132
representatives of
Church of Norway 89; Indigenous
nations 142, 153, 156
repression 13, 19, 25, 48, 69, 80
resistance 57, 119
rituals of 11–30
resolution (of conflict) 118, 132
resource
dance as 6, 115–135; rituals as 11, 25,
93, 150; self-development as 115

restrictions
freedom 13; speech 53
revelation 127, 135, 146
Revelations, Book of 83
revitalization 107, 149, 152
revolutionary
energy 37; France 56; potential of
effervescence 38; Revolutionary
Muslims 17
rhythms
celestial bodies 83; dance 6, 115–135;
water 82
Riddu Riđđu
festival 7, 150–153, 155; mountains 150
rights 50, 55, 59, 118, 140–141
animal 68; free speech 52; human 14,
20–21, 23; Indigenous 148; to criticize
26, 58; to protest 34, 50; violations 14,
54, 101
risk 22, 32, 33, 82, 101
rites 38, 143
Dionysian 40; energy release 40;
magical 2; religious 36; totemic 36, 39
ritual, rituals 1–7, 11, 12, 14, 16, 18, 20,
22–24, 26–28, 31–33, 35–41, 43–45,
48–64, 67, 68, 70, 72–80, 82, 84,
86, 88–90, 93–98, 100, 102, 104–12,
115–116, 118–20, 122, 124, 126, 128,
130, 132, 134–140, 142, 144, 146–48,
150, 152–54, 156
acts or performances 1, 2, 4; as
mobilizer 1–3; as a resource 11, 25,
93, 150; complex 67, 72, 74; dance,
movement, rhythms 134; experiments
97; for inter-cultural exchanges155;
How To Do Things With 93–111;
liturgical 70; mourning 55; of food
5; of hospitality and tourism 72; of
pilgrims and pilgrimage 68, 74, 90;
of resistance and struggle 11–29,
50, 52, 55; performativity of 51;
perlocutionary and illocutionary 51;
politically subversive 50; protests (*see*
under protests); religious 88; role in
democratization 7; social effectiveness
of 90
ritualistic dimension
to social movements 51; to solidarity
54

www.ingramcontent.com/pod-product-compliance
Lightning Source LLC
Chambersburg PA
CBHW050714280326
41926CB00088B/3021